ACTS OF WORSHIP FOR ASSEMBLIES

By the same author:
After Confirmation
Assemblies for School and Children's Church
Assembly Themes
More Assembly Services

ACTS OF WORSHIP FOR ASSEMBLIES

by
R. H. LLOYD

Chaplain of The Dragon School, Oxford
Fellows' Chaplain of Magdalen College, Oxford

MOWBRAY
LONDON & OXFORD

First published 1982 by A. R. Mowbray & Co. Ltd.,
Saint Thomas House, Becket Street,
Oxford, OX1 1SJ

Phototypeset by Cotswold Typesetting Ltd., Cheltenham

Printed in Great Britain by Biddles of Guildford

TO: HAZEL, CATHERINE AND SIMON

CONTENTS

PREFACE

A few months before he died, Ian Ramsay, a former bishop of Durham, delivered a lecture to a meeting of school chaplains at Bloxham. During the course of the lecture he laid emphasis on the importance of collecting 'modern' parables to shed light on the old.

The 'story' has been used from time immemorial as a vehicle for communicating concepts and truths. In any gathering of people, e.g., a school assembly or a church congregation, there must be a wide spread of IQs., and it must follow that it is difficult to pitch what you have to say so that all will benefit. The wonderful thing about a story is that each person can slot in at his or her particular level. I like to think that Jesus was conscious of this and deliberately used stories to convey his truths, knowing that the dullest person would grasp something about the Kingdom of Heaven, and at the same time challenging the most intellectual Pharisee present to plumb their depths.

A good story quickens the imagination and creates a sense of wonder and awe. We must never forget that imagination is the vehicle for conveying truth, and it is truth that brings us to the brink of worship and the moment of disclosure.

'Man lives not only by arguments but also by stories. Not only by concepts but also by images. He *needs* valid images and stories that can be retold.'

When I arrived at The Dragon School in 1969 I inherited a form of service I found to be ideally suited for young people, and I have done little to alter it. It is a 'thematic' service and calls for two biblical and two secular readings. Whereas it is relatively easy to find two biblical passages to suit a theme, it is more difficult to find a supply of secular passages week by week. Happily, I also inherited the tradition of inviting lots of visiting preachers and speakers, and I have taken every opportunity of inviting them to choose their readings – particularly the secular readings! This has meant that I have had access to a rich quarry of material.

This book embraces a wider age range than do my former books in that some of the 'readings' are more geared to an older age group.

You will see that as well as giving the biblical reference, I have quoted at some length from the passage, because I have found it helpful to do so. Unless I have a Bible to hand and because I do not have a photographic memory, a simple reference is often irritatingly meaningless. As you will see, I have used the NEB translation, but that is a personal choice, as yours must be.

It has been most encouraging to learn from so many quarters that my Assembly books have proved to be useful, not only to teachers but also to those who have to prepare addresses for children's services in church.

What does strike me, however, is the fact that there must be an enormous number of excellent stories tucked away in countless brains. If you happen to have such a story, and if you are prepared to share it, I would be delighted to hear from you.

R. H. LLOYD
The Dragon School
Oxford

A PRAYER FOR
THE SCHOOL

O God, make the door of this school wide enough to receive all who need human love and fellowship; and narrow enough to shut out all envy, pride and strife.

Make its threshold smooth enough to be no stumbling block to children, nor to straying feet, but rugged and strong enough to turn back the tempter's power. God make the door of this school the gateway to thine eternal kingdom.

(A prayer found in the ruins of St Stephen's, Walbrook, London.

Slightly amended)

1

JUDGING OTHERS

Aim: There is hardly anyone who has not been guilty of some grave misjudgement; there is hardly anyone who has not suffered from someone else's misjudgement. And yet the strange fact is that there is hardly any commandment of Jesus which is more consistently broken and neglected. It is almost impossible for any man to be strictly impartial in his judgement. Again and again we are swayed by our instinctive and unreasoning reactions to people.

Illustration:
Mrs Boyd-Gregor was the wife of a prosperous farmer and lived on the outskirts of the little Cotswold village of Milton-on-the-Wold. Each Thursday morning she boarded the 10.15 train to do her shopping in the nearby market town of Throckleton.

One warm Thursday morning she boarded the train and settled comfortably into her favourite seat next to the window. She enjoyed sitting there because it gave her an excellent view of what the local farmers were doing.

On the seat opposite Mrs Boyd-Gregor sat a frail, poorly dressed, elderly lady, with a shopping basket on the seat beside her. The two women exchanged smiles, commented briefly on the closeness of the weather and sank back into their own thoughts.

As the train chuffed its way leisurely through the countryside, its soothing gentle rhythm soon lulled Mrs Boyd-Gregor to sleep. She woke up with a start as the train drew to a stop, but she relaxed just as swiftly when she noted that they had only reached the tiny station of Ashdown Major. She smiled to herself when she saw that her aged travelling companion had also dozed off.

Mrs Boyd-Gregor opened her handbag and reached inside for her mirror. As she did so, she casually glanced at the side pocket where she usually kept her bank notes. To her horror, she saw that the pocket was empty! There should have been ten crisp ~~one~~ *five*-pound notes there; the housekeeping money her husband had given her yesterday.

Swiftly she checked through all the other pockets and compartments of her large handbag, but there was no trace of the money. She even emptied all the contents of her bag on to the seat beside her, just to be absolutely sure, but the money simply was not there. What could have happened to it? Where could it possibly have gone? It couldn't just disappear into thin air! How was she to do her shopping without money?

As she sat there pondering on her predicament her eyes fell on the old woman sitting opposite, still fast asleep.

'I wonder!' she thought to herself. 'Could that old lady have opened my handbag and taken it whilst I slept!'

Mrs Boyd-Gregor was ashamed of herself for having allowed such an unworthy thought to cross her mind. She tried to dismiss it from her thoughts, but the suspicion persisted. The thought came back.

'Could the old lady have taken it? After all, she looks very poor and shabby!'

Mrs Boyd-Gregor looked at the woman's worn and ancient overcoat and noticed a purse just peeping out of one of the pockets.

'Well, there's only one way of finding out,' she thought to herself. And, acting on impulse, hardly daring to breathe, she leaned across and very gently removed the old woman's purse. Swiftly she opened it and looked inside. There, sure enough, lying amongst a few copper coins, carefully folded, were a number of crisp, new ~~one~~ _five_-pound notes. She counted them; there were ten!

Now what was she to do? Should she wake the old lady and confront her with her theft? She decided against that immediately because she did not like scenes.

Should she summon the ticket collector and place the whole matter in his hands? She decided against that course of action as well, because it would inevitably lead to a prosecution, and Mrs Boyd-Gregor didn't much relish the idea of having to appear in court to give evidence.

She decided instead to take the matter into her own hands, and in any case, she thought, it would be the kindest and most compassionate solution to the problem. She removed the _five_ pound notes and put them into her handbag and gently returned the purse into the old lady's pocket.

Leaning back and relaxing once more, Mrs Boyd-Gregor felt very pleased with herself. After all, she had retrieved her money and that was the important thing.

The train drew into Throckleton and Mrs Boyd-Gregor left the compartment. She noticed that the old lady was awake and staring out of the window. Clearly she was travelling to a further destination.

2

That evening when Mrs Boyd-Gregor arrived back at Milton-on-the-Wold, her husband was waiting for her on the station platform. He greeted her with his usual smile and kiss, and taking the heavy shopping bag, inquired how the day had gone.

'Very well, thank you, my dear,' she replied. 'But I must tell you what happened to me on the train this morning. I just happened to open my handbag to reach for my mirror when I noticed. . . .'

Before she could continue, her husband interrupted her – 'I know what happened,' he said, 'you discovered that you had left your housekeeping money behind. When I got back home after taking you to the station, the first thing I saw on the kitchen table was the bundle of five pound notes. Tell me,' he continued, 'where did you get the money from to do your shopping?'

READINGS:

St Matthew 5.8. 'How blest are those whose hearts are pure; they shall see God.'

St Matthew 7.1,2. 'Pass no judgement, and you will not be judged. For as you judge others, so you will yourselves be judged, and whatever measure you deal out to others will be dealt back to you.'

PRAYER:

Whatsoever things are true and just,
Whatsoever things are pure and lovely,
Whatsoever things are gentle and generous,
    honourable, and of good report;
These things, O Lord, grant that we may with
    one accord pursue, for Jesus Christ's sake. *Amen.*

God be in my head,
    And in my understanding;
God be in mine eyes,
    And in my looking;
God be in my mouth,
    And in my speaking;
God be in my heart,
    And in my thinking;
God be at my end,
    And at my departing.
                Amen.

The Lord's Prayer.

HYMNS: *Blest are the pure in heart.*
        Awake, my soul, and with the sun.

3

THE GOLDEN RULE

Aim: It is a lesson that everyone should learn sooner than later, namely, that generally speaking, people tend to react towards us as we behave towards them.

'The fault, dear Brutus, is not in our stars,
But in ourselves. . . . '

(*Julius Caesar, Act 1, Scene 2*)

Illustration:

The philosopher Socrates was resting in the shade of a large olive tree one hot afternoon, when he was approached by a traveller, making his way towards Athens.

'Tell me!' said the traveller, 'What sort of people live in Athens?'

Socrates looked up at him and replied, 'Where do you come from?'

'I come from Argos,' he answered.

'What are the people like in Argos?' asked Socrates.

'Awful!' he exclaimed. 'They're a lot of quarrelsome, unsociable, lying layabouts.'

Socrates pondered awhile as he studied the man, and then said very slowly, 'I'm sorry to tell you, but you'll find the people of Athens just the same.'

Presently another traveller came by and asked a similar question. Again Socrates inquired where he came from.

'I come from Argos,' came the reply.

'What are the people like there?' asked Socrates.

'Charming!' answered the traveller. 'The people of Argos are kind, gentle, friendly, honest and hardworking.'

Socrates smiled and said, 'I am pleased to tell you, my friend, that you'll find the people of Athens are much the same.'

READINGS:

St Matthew 7. 1-13. '. . . For as you judge others, so you will yourselves be judged. . . . Why do you look at the speck of sawdust in your brother's eye, with never a thought for the great plank in your own? . . . . Ask and you will receive; seek, and you will find. . . . Always treat others as you would like them to treat you: that is the Law and the prophets.'

Romans 12. 9-21. 'Love in all sincerity. . . . Let love for our brotherhood breed warmth of mutual affection. Give pride of place to one another in esteem. . . . Let hope keep you joyful, in trouble stand firm; persist in prayer. Contribute to the needs of God's people, and practise hospitality. . . . Care as much about each other as about yourselves. . . . Do not let evil conquer you, but use good to defeat evil.'

PRAYER:

Help us, O God, at all times to act towards others as we would wish them to act towards us.

Help us,
To make the same allowances for others as we would wish them to make for us;
To be as sympathetic and understanding to others as we would wish them to be to us;
To encourage others as we would wish them to encourage us;
To help others as we would wish them to help us;
To be as just and fair to others as we would wish them to be to us;
To forgive others as we would wish them to forgive us.
Before we criticize others, help us to remember what it feels like to be criticized.
Before we find fault with others, help us to remember what it feels like to be found fault with.
Before we condemn others, help us to remember what it feels like to be condemned.
Help us at all times to be like Jesus,
Who went about doing good;
Who was among men as one who serves;
Who even on the Cross prayed that his enemies should be forgiven.
Amen.

(William Barclay)

The Lord's Prayer.

HYMNS: *Give me joy in my heart, keep me praising.*
O thou who camest from above.

5

3

THE ART OF PERSUASION

Aim: How much readier people are to listen when we temper what we have to say with love and sensitivity.

Illustration:
The wind and the sun were arguing over which of them was the stronger. As they argued they saw a traveller making his way across the plain below them.

'I'll tell you what!' exclaimed the wind, 'whichever one of us succeeds in stripping the cloak off that traveller let him be acknowledged as the stronger.' The sun accepted the challenge.

'And since the idea was mine,' continued the wind, 'I'll have first go.'

So saying, the wind swept down upon the traveller and blew gust after gust at him, whipping fiercely at the cloak; but only succeeded in persuading the traveller to wrap his cloak more firmly around himself. The wind built up the pressure, and hurled itself across the plain, whistling and howling as it attempted to tear away the offending garment. But the harder it blew, the tighter became the traveller's grip. In the end, utterly exhausted, the wind blew itself out, and gave up.

'Watch this!' smiled the sun. 'It's quite easy really.' And turning towards the traveller, it released a few warm gentle rays, and then, very gradually turned up the heat. The traveller responded immediately. First of all he loosened his cloak to cool himself, and then, greatly perspiring, took it off altogether.

READINGS:
> *Proverbs 15. 1-4.*
> 'A soft answer turns away anger,
> but a sharp word makes tempers hot.
> A wise man's tongue spreads knowledge:
> stupid men talk nonsense.
>
> A soothing word is a staff of life
> but a mischievous tongue breaks the spirit.'

> *St Matthew 5. 25-26.* 'If someone sues you, come to terms with him promptly. . . ; otherwise he may hand you over to the judge. . . .'

St Matthew 5. 38-42. 'You have learned that they were told, "Eye for eye, tooth for tooth." But what I tell you is this: Do not set yourself against the man who wrongs you. If someone slaps you on the right cheek, turn and offer him your left. If a man wants to sue you for your shirt, let him have your coat as well. If a man in authority makes you go one mile, go with him two. . . .'

St John 15. 12. 'This is my commandment: love one another, as I have loved you.'

PRAYER:
O God,
　　Teach us the value of tact and discretion; may we know when silence is better than speech; help us to refrain from speaking harsh words. Give us sensitivity to the needs of others and grace to reflect the love of Jesus in our lives.

Amen.

The Lord's Prayer.

HYMNS: *Take my life and let it be.*
　　　　O thou not made with hands.

4

DIFFERENCES

Aim: The truth of a matter is often multi-faceted like those slowly revolving multi-mirrored globes of by-gone ballrooms. In any debate, argument or discussion, therefore, no single person should try to impose his will on the rest. Each should listen to what the rest have to say, and in this way freely achieve a 'common mind'.

Illustration:
On one of his many journeys the Buddha happened to be staying in the region of Savatthi. Here he came across a number of holy men who were arguing fiercely with one another, each claiming that his point of view was the true one. When they saw the Buddha, they asked him to judge

7

between them. The Buddha agreed to do this and patiently listened as each man presented his case. Presently when everyone had had his say, the Buddha told them the following story:

'In former times, brethren, there was a Raja of this place who commanded one of his servants to gather to him all the blind men of Savatthi. When this was done the Raja said, "O ye blind men, such as this is an elephant," and he showed them one by one the elephant.

'And to one he presented the head of the elephant, to another the ear, to another a tusk, the trunk, the foot, tail and tuft of the tail, saying to each, "Such as this is an elephant."

'When he had finished, the Raja went to the blind men and said to each: "Have you studied the elephant?"

' "Yes, your Majesty," they replied.

' "Then tell me your conclusions about him."

'Thereupon those who had been presented with the head answered, "Your Majesty, an elephant is just like a pot." And those who had only observed the ear replied, "An elephant is just like a winnowing fan." Those who had been presented with the tusk said it was a ploughshare, those who knew only the trunk said it was a serpent. "The body," said they, "is a granary: the foot, a pillar: the tail, a pestle: the tuft of the tail, just a broom."

'Then they began to quarrel, shouting, "Yes, it is!" "No, it isn't!" "An elephant is not like that!" "Yes, it is like that!" and so on until they came to fighting about the matter.

'Then, brethren, the Raja was delighted with the scene.

' "Such folk," said the Exalted one, "can learn nothing about the form of Truth, except the little part that has been presented to them." '

READINGS:

1 Corinthians 1. 10-28. 'I appeal to you, my brothers, in the name of our Lord Jesus Christ: agree among yourselves, and avoid divisions; be firmly joined in unity of mind and thought. I have been told. . . . each of you is saying, "I am Paul's man," or "I am for Apollos"; "I follow Cephas", or "I am Christ's." Surely Christ has not been divided among you?'

1 Corinthians 12. 4-27. 'There are varieties of gifts, but the same Spirit. There are varieties of service, but the same Lord. There are many forms of work. . . . In each of us the Spirit is manifested in one particular way, for some useful purpose. . . . A body is not one single organ, but many. . . . Now you are Christ's body, and each of you a limb or organ of it.'

8

PRAYER:
O God,
Give us wisdom which is open to reason.
Give us a sense of proportion to see the things which really
matter.
Save us from that arrogance, which makes us think that it is
only our opinion which really matters.
Save us from prejudice which cannot hear or see another's
point of view.
And help us not to spoil our own case by trying to ram it
down someone's throat.
O God, grant that your Holy Spirit may in all things direct and
rule our hearts, through Jesus Christ our Lord.
                    Amen.

The Lord's Prayer.

HYMNS: *God is love: his the care.*
God be in my head, and in my understanding.

5

GIVING

Aim: 'I expect to pass through this world but once. Any good thing,
therefore, that I can do, or any kindness that I can show any
fellow creature, let me do it now. Let me not defer, or neglect it,
for I shall not pass this way again.' (*Anon*)
The Duke of Edinburgh once said, 'Life is like a bucket, the more
you put into it, the more you get out of it.'

Illustration:
I had gone a-begging from door to door in the village path, when thy
golden chariot appeared in the distance like a gorgeous dream and I
wondered who was this King of all Kings!
My hopes rose high and methought my evil days were at an end and I
stood waiting for alms to be given unasked and for wealth to be scattered
on all sides in the dust.

The chariot stopped where I stood. Thy glance fell on me and thou camest down with a smile. I felt that the luck of my life had come at last. Then of a sudden thou didst hold out thy right hand and say, 'What hast thou to give me?'

Ah what a kingly jest was it to open thy palm to a beggar to beg! I was confused and stood undecided, and then from my wallet I slowly took out one least little grain of corn and gave it to thee.

But how great was my surprise when at the day's end I emptied my bag on the floor to find a least little grain of gold among my poor heap. I bitterly wept and wished that I had had the heart to give thee my all.

(Rabindranath Tagore, Gitanjali)

READINGS:

> *St Mark 14. 3-9.* 'Jesus was at Bethany. . . . As he sat at table, a woman came in carrying a small bottle of very costly perfume, pure oil of nard. She broke it open and poured the oil over his head. . . . Let her alone. . . . It is a fine thing she has done for me. . . . I tell you this: wherever in all the world the Gospel is proclaimed, what she has done will be told as her memorial.'

> *2 Corinthians 9. 6–8.* 'Remember: sparse sowing, sparse reaping; sow bountifully, and you will reap bountifully. Each person should give as he has decided for himself; there should be no reluctance, no sense of compulsion; God loves a cheerful giver. . . .'

PRAYER:

> Holy Father,
> Help us to remember that all things come from you, and that of your own do we give you.
> Keep us from being selfish in the use of the gifts and possessions you have given us.
> Help us always to give and share, and never to keep and hold.
> Help us to follow the example of your Son, who gave generously of his care, his time and his gifts, and did not hesitate to give his life on the cross for our redemption.
> Help us, O God, to be generous and never selfish, so that we may follow faithfully in the footsteps of our Lord and Master, the very pattern of our lives, Jesus Christ.
> *Amen.*

> The Lord's Prayer.

HYMNS: *O Lord of heaven and earth and sea.*
When I survey the wondrous cross.

10

6

THE WRONG USE OF THE TONGUE

Aim: The tongue can be the bully's most lethal instrument, inflicting far more pain and unhappiness than any fist or whip.

It isn't so much what we say, as the manner in which we say it. The most innocent utterance can take on a variety of meanings when accompanied by a raised eyebrow, a knowing wink, or a sneer; and if these were not enough the tone of voice can broaden the spectrum.

That is why rumour can be so insidious. Often times when we trace a rumour back to its very source, we find nothing more than an apparently innocent utterance, but no longer accompanied by its original inflection and hooded eye.

Lord, remind us often that a gossip's mouth is the devil's mailbag.
(Welsh Proverb)

Whispered insinuations are the rhetoric of the devil.
(J. W. Von Goethe)

The slanderous tongue kills three;
the slandered, the slanderer, and him who listens to the slander.
(The Talmud)

Illustration:
When Archbishop Theobald died, Henry II used his influence to have his Chancellor, Thomas Becket, appointed as the new Archbishop of Canterbury, hoping thereby to bring the Church in England under the royal jurisdiction. His plan backfired on him. Thomas, who whilst Chancellor had been the king's man, now became the uncompromising champion of the Church. This led to a head-on clash between the king and the Archbishop.

The quarrel between them grew so bitter that Becket on one occasion had to flee to France for safety.

After an exile of six years, Becket was asked to return by the king. He was received rapturously by the common people who knelt at the roadside to ask his blessing as he made his way from Sandwich to Canterbury.

One of the first things the Archbishop did on his return, was to discipline those bishops who had obeyed the king in his absence. At the time when Henry heard about this, he happened to be attending a banquet in a castle in Normandy. His anger blazed and he shouted!

'Who will rid me of this troublesome priest?'

Immediately, four of his knights left the banqueting chamber, crossed the Channel, and headed for Canterbury. On the night of 29 December 1170, they slew Becket on the altar steps of his cathedral and fled into the night.

The whole of Europe was horrified by this callous crime and the king shut himself away in his room for three days, weeping and praying for forgiveness, declaring that it was not what he had wanted. When he returned, he showed his sorrow for what he had done, by walking barefooted to Canterbury to pray at Becket's tomb and submitting his bare back to be lashed with knotted thongs.

(It is possible that Henry had no intention of harming Becket. We shall never know because there is no way of recapturing the expression on his face or the tone of his voice when he uttered those historic words. *'Who will rid me of this troublesome priest?'*)

READINGS:

Ecclesiasticus 28. 13–21 and 24–26.

'Curses on the gossip and the tale-bearer!
For they have been the ruin of many peaceable men.
The talk of a third party has wrecked the lives of many
and driven them from country to country;
it has destroyed fortified towns
and demolished the houses of the great.
The talk of a third party has brought divorce on staunch wives
and deprived them of all they have laboured for.
Whoever pays heed to it will never again find rest
or live in peace of mind.
The lash of a whip raises weals,
but the lash of a tongue breaks bones.
Many have been killed by the sword,
but not so many as by the tongue.
Happy the man who is sheltered from its onslaught,
who has not been exposed to its fury,
who has not borne its yoke,
or been chained with its fetters!
For its yoke is of iron,
its fetters of bronze.
The death it brings is an evil death;
better the grave than the tongue!. . . .'

'As you enclose your garden with a thorn hedge,
and lock up your silver and gold,
so weigh your words and measure them,
and make a door and a bolt for your mouth.
Beware of being tripped by your tongue
and falling into the power of a lurking enemy.'

St Mark 7. 31–37. 'They brought to him a man who was deaf and
had an impediment in his speech, with the request that he would
lay his hand on him. He . . . put his fingers into his ears, spat, and
touched his tongue. Then, looking up to heaven, he sighed, and
said to him, *"Ephphatha,"* which means "Be opened." With
that his ears were opened, and at the same time. . . he spoke
plainly.'

James 3. 2–12. 'All of us often go wrong; the man who never says
a wrong thing is a perfect character, able to bridle his whole being.
If we put bits into horses' mouths to make them obey our will, we
can direct their whole body. Or think of ships: large they may be,
yet even when driven by strong gales they can be directed by a tiny
rudder on whatever course the helmsman chooses. So with the
tongue. It is a small member but it can make huge claims.
      'What an immense stack of timber can be set ablaze by the
tiniest spark! And the tongue is in effect a fire. It represents
among our members the world with all its wickedness; it pollutes
our whole being; it keeps the wheel of our existence red-hot, and
its flames are fed by hell. Beasts and birds of every kind, creatures
that crawl on the ground or swim in the sea, can be subdued and
have been subdued by mankind; but no man can subdue the
tongue. It is an intractable evil, charged with deadly venom. We
use it to sing praises of our Lord and Father, and we use it to
invoke curses upon our fellow-men who are made in God's
likeness. Out of the same mouth come praises and curses. My
brothers, this should not be so. Does a fountain gush with both
fresh and brackish water from the same opening? Can a fig-tree,
my brothers, yield olives, or a vine figs? No more does salt water
yield fresh.'

PRAYER:
      Set a watch, O Lord, upon our tongue,
      that we may never speak the cruel word which is untrue;
      or, being true, is not the whole truth;

13

or, being wholly true, is merciless;
for the love of Jesus Christ our Lord. *Amen.*

Holy Father, we remember that your Son Jesus Christ sighed before he restored the gift of speech to the dumb. May we ever respect this gift and never put it to a wrong use. Give us such control over our tongues that what we say may be tempered with love, truthfulness, sincerity and purity. *Amen.*

The Lord's Prayer.

HYMNS: *O Jesus, I have promised.*
If I had a hammer, I'd hammer in the morning.

7

GOD'S TEMPLES

Aim: To remind ourselves that we are God's living temples. That God not only dwells in us, but in our fellow-men as well. If we wish to see God, we must look into the eyes of a fellow-being. We are sanctuaries of God's Holy Spirit and channels of his grace.

Illustration:
Once upon a time, or rather at the birth of Time, when the gods were so new that they had no names, and Man was still damp from the clay of the pit whence he had been digged, Man claimed that he, too, was some sort of god.

The gods weighed his evidence, and decided that Man's claim was good. Having conceded Man's claim, the legend goes that they came by stealth and stole away his godhead, with intent to hide it where Man should never find it again, but this was not easy. If they hid it anywhere on Earth the gods foresaw that Man would leave no stone unturned till he had recovered it. If they concealed it among themselves they feared Man might batter his way up even to the skies.

And while they were thus at a stand, the wisest of the gods said, 'I know. Give it to me!' He closed his hand upon the tiny, unstable light of Man's stolen godhead, and when that great hand opened again the light

14

was gone. 'All is well,' said Brahm. 'I have hidden it where Man will never dream of looking for it. I have hidden it inside Man himself.'

(Rudyard Kipling)

READINGS:

Genesis 2. 7. 'Then the Lord God formed a man from the dust of the ground and breathed into his nostrils the breath of life. Thus the man became a living creature.'

St Matthew 25. 31–46. '. . . when I was hungry, you gave me food; when thirsty, you gave me drink. . . . I tell you this: anything you did for one of my brothers here, however humble, you did for me. . . .'

1 Corinthians 3. 16, 17. 'Surely you know that you are God's temple, where the Spirit of God dwells. Anyone who destroys God's temple will himself be destroyed by God, because the temple of God is holy; and that temple you are.'

1 Corinthians 6. 19. 'Do you not know that your body is a shrine of the indwelling Holy Spirit, and the Spirit is God's gift to you? You do not belong to yourselves; you were bought at a price. Then honour God in your body.'

Revelation 21. 3. (AV) '. . . the tabernacle of God is with men.'

PRAYER:

Christ has no body now
    on earth but yours.
No hands but yours,
No feet but yours;
Yours are the eyes
    through which is to look out
Christ's compassion to the World;
Yours are the feet
    with which he is
    to go about doing good;
Yours are the hands
    with which he is
    to bless us now. *Amen.*

The Lord's Prayer.

HYMNS: *Come, Holy Ghost, our souls inspire.*
    Our blest Redeemer, ere he breathed.

8

STEWARDSHIP

Aim: Material possessions tend to fix a man's heart to this world and make it difficult for him to think beyond it. Dr Johnson was once shown round a famous castle and its lovely grounds. After he had seen it all, he turned to his friends and said, 'These are the things that make it difficult to die.'

Illustration:
King Midas of Phrygia welcomed Silenus (a satyr) to his palace and honoured him with a great banquet. As he departed, Silenus turned to the king and said, 'In return for your generous hospitality, I am prepared to grant you one wish. You have but to ask, and it will be granted.' Midas considered the offer carefully and then replied, 'I wish that everything I touch will be turned into gold.'

'Your wish is granted,' came the reply.

The king tested the good faith of Silenus by touching this and that, and could scarcely believe his own senses when he broke a green twig from a low-growing branch of oak, and the twig turned to gold. He lifted a stone from the ground and the stone, likewise, gleamed pale gold. He touched a sod of earth and the earth, by the power of his touch, became a lump of ore. The dry ears of corn which he gathered were a harvest of golden metal, and when he plucked an apple from a tree and held it in his hand, you would have thought that it was an apple of gold. If he laid his finger on the pillars of his lofty doorways, they were seen to shine and glitter, and even when he washed his hands in clear water, the trickles that flowed over his palms became a golden shower. He dreamed of everything turned to gold, and his hopes soared beyond the limits of his imagination.

So he exulted in his good fortune, while servants set before him tables piled high with meats, and with bread in abundance. But then, when he touched a piece of bread, it grew stiff and hard; if he hungrily tried to bite into the meat, a sheet of gold encased the food, as soon as his teeth came in contact with it. He took some wine, and adding clear water, mixed himself a drink; the liquid could be seen turned to molten gold as it passed his lips. He lifted a bunch of grapes to his mouth, but they turned into golden balls gleaming and glowing, but impossible to eat.

As the days went by his despair and hunger grew. He could not sleep or eat. When he embraced his children, they turned instantly into golden figures.

16

In desparation he consulted the oracle; the advice he was given gave him hope.

'Go at once to the river Pactobus and bathe in its waters.'

Midas obeyed the oracle and bathed himself in the river. The curse was immediately lifted and from that day to this the sands of the Pactobus have yielded grains of gold.

READINGS:

St Mark 10. 17–27. '. . . a stranger ran up, and, kneeling before him, asked, "Good Master, what must I do to win eternal life?". . . . ". . . go, sell everything you have, and give to the poor, and you will have riches in heaven; and come, follow me." At these words his face fell and he went away with a heavy heart; for he was a man of great wealth.'

1 Timothy 6. 7–11. 'We brought nothing into the world; for that matter we cannot take anything with us when we leave. . . . The love of money is the root of all evil things.'

PRAYER:

Dear God,

Help us to be good stewards of our time, our talents
    and our wealth.
Help us to use life wisely and not foolishly,
    to use life generously and not selfishly.
Give us at all times a right understanding of the nature
    of money,
And grant that we may always remember that one day we shall
    have to give an account to you.

To that end help us always to walk with Jesus who is the Lord of all good life and who came to give us life and life more abundantly. *Amen.*

The Lord's Prayer.

HYMNS: *Lord of all power, I give you my will.*
    Be thou my vision, O Lord of my heart.

9

WATCH!

Aim: It is by constant vigilance and discipline over our personal lives that we shall keep our spiritual lives healthy and in good repair.

It is only by constant vigilance and a lot of effort that we shall keep our nation healthy. We should be ready and willing to become involved in matters that concern us, for example, local council work, the local magistrates' bench, our trade union branch. If we don't, others will!

Illustration:

In the middle of Sri Lanka there is a place where great temples and palaces were discovered recently, hidden in dense jungle. They had been built two thousand years ago and had belonged to a Ceylonese empire which some of the wisest historians say was as great as the empires of Greece and Rome. And yet only a few years ago practically nobody had any idea that they were there at all! The jungle had covered them all up, and what were once towns, with crowds and all the bustle of life, had become the 'buried cities', as they were called.

A famous Ceylonese historian was asked how it had happened. 'Oh,' he said, 'there are a number of possible reasons; some say that a dreadful disease such as cholera killed so many of the people that the rest just ran away in terror; others think that these cities were invaded by enemies who looted them and took the people off into slavery. But,' he went on, 'I personally think there's a simpler reason. I think the people became lazy and careless so that it was too much trouble for them to bother about the jungle which was like a great weed in their garden. And so the day came when there was no garden; it was all weed and the jungle had won.'

(Donald O. Soper)

READINGS:

Proverbs 6. 6–11. 'Go to the ant, you sluggard, watch her ways and get wisdom. . . . A little sleep, a little slumber, a little folding of the hands in rest, and poverty will come upon you like a robber, want like a ruffian.'

St Matthew 25. 1–13. '. . . There were ten girls, who took their lamps and went out to meet the bridegroom. . . . As the bridegroom was late in coming they all dozed off to sleep. But at midnight a cry was heard: "Here is the bridegroom! Come out to

18

meet him''. . . . Keep awake then; for you never know the day or the hour.'

Ephesians 6. 10–20. 'Finally then, find your strength in the Lord . . . . Put on all the armour which God provides, so that you may be able to stand firm against the devices of the devil. . . . Fasten on the belt of truth; for coat of mail put on integrity; let the shoes on your feet be the gospel of peace, to give you firm footing; and, with all these, take the great shield of faith. . . . Take salvation for helmet; for sword, take that which the Spirit gives you – the words that come from God. . . . To this end keep watch and persevere. . .'

PRAYER:

O God, our Creator and our Father, it is you who gave us life.
Now teach us how to use life.
When we are thinking and planning what to do with life,
    help us to have the right kind of ambition.
Help us to think
    Not of how much we can get out of life, but of how much we
        can put into life;
Not of how much we can get, but of how much we can give;
Not of the number of people we can use, but of the number of
        people to whom we can be of use.
Help us,
    Not to be the kind of people who are always remembering
        their rights and always forgetting their duties;
    Not to be the kind of people who want to get everything out
        of life and to put nothing into it;
    Not to be the kind of people who do not care what happens
        to others so long as they are all right.
Help us at all times to remember our responsibility to you.
Help us,
    To remember that we shall answer to you for the way we
        have used the gifts you gave us;
    To remember that we shall give account for all that we have
        been allotted in this life;
    To remember at all times how you have loved us and how
        Jesus died for us. *Amen.*

(*William Barclay*)

The Lord's Prayer.

HYMNS: *Stand up, stand up for Jesus.*
       Ye servants of the Lord.

WORRY AND REGRET

Aim: So often we spoil the present by regretting the past. We regret our missed chances and lost opportunities (the Tiger of the Past!). 'If only I had. . . !' Oftentimes we spoil the present by worrying about what may happen tomorrow, next week, next month or next year (the Tiger of the Future!). How much wiser it is to take each day as it comes; putting the past behind us and not being anxious about the future.
'Yesterday is but a dream
And tomorrow is only a vision;
But today well lived
Makes every yesterday a dream of happiness,
And every tomorrow a vision of hope.
Look well, therefore, to this day!
Such is the salutation of the dawn.'

(from India)

Illustration:
The Buddha tells the following story:
'There was a man who was being hotly pursued along a jungle path by a ferocious tiger, when suddenly, he came to the edge of a precipice. Fortunately there happened to be a vine growing over the edge; without hesitating to look over his shoulder the man swiftly grasped the vine and lowered himself down, hand over hand, to safety. As he reached half-way, he happened to glance downwards, when to his horror he saw another tiger prowling around beneath him.

In desperation he jerked his head upwards, the sight that met his eyes made him shiver with horror. Not only did he see the first tiger's gaping jaws, but he also saw a mouse busily gnawing away at the vine on which he was hanging.

As he hung there in desperate plight he noticed a large, red, ripe strawberry growing out of a fissure near his elbow. The man carefully picked it, and placing it slowly in his mouth, closed his eyes and savoured its lovely flavour to the full.'

READING:
St Matthew 6. 25-34. 'Therefore I bid you put away anxious thoughts. . . . Set your mind on God's kingdom and his justice

before everything else, and all the rest shall come to you as well.
So do not be anxious about tomorrow; tomorrow will look after
itself. Each day has troubles enough of its own.'

Heavenly Father,
Inspire us with heavenly thoughts;
Pardon what is past;
Rectify what is present;
Order what is to come.
Give us,
Serenity to accept what cannot be changed;
Courage to change what should be changed;
And wisdom to distinguish the one from the other:
through Jesus Christ our Lord. *Amen.*

The Lord's Prayer.

HYMNS: *Put thou thy trust in God.*
O for a closer walk with God.

11

'LOOK TO THE ROCK FROM WHICH YOU WERE HEWN'
(Isaiah 51.1)

Aim: 'Jesus replied, "I am the way; I am the truth and I am life". . . .'
(St John 14.6)
We do well to remember this, surrounded as we are by shrilly
proclaimed alternatives.

Illustration:
There was a spider who lived high up in the roof of a barn. Since there
were very few flies at that height he decided to try his luck further down.
To this end, the spider spun a thick thread, and attaching it to a wooden
lath, lowered himself into space. Eventually he reached a great crossbeam
and decided to seek his fortune at that level. He carefully constructed a
large web and settled down to wait. He had chosen well! He caught
dozens of flies and soon grew fat and sleek.

21

One day in the process of repairing his web he stumbled over one of the principal threads which stretched upwards into the darkness.

'What an awkwardly situated thread this is!' the spider muttered to himself. 'I could easily trip over and fall down to the barn floor and injure myself. I don't really need it any more anyway.'

So he gave the offending thread a big bite and severed it. As he did so, he brought down the magnificent web in complete ruin around his ears.

READINGS:

1 Corinthians 1. 18–31. 'This doctrine of the cross is sheer folly to those on their way to ruin, but to us who are on the way to salvation it is the power of God. . . .'

2 Thessalonians 2. 13–17. 'Stand firm, then, brothers, and hold fast to the traditions which you have learned from us by word or by letter. And may our Lord Jesus Christ himself and God our Father, who has shown us such love, and in his grace has given us such unfailing encouragement and such bright hopes, still encourage and fortify you in every good deed and word!'

2 Timothy 3. 14–17. 'But for your part, stand by the truths you have learned and are assured of. Remember from whom you learned them; remember that from early childhood you have been familiar with the sacred writings which have power to make you wise and lead you to salvation through faith in Christ Jesus.'

PRAYER:

Blessed Lord, you have caused the holy Scriptures to be written for our learning:

Grant that we may hear them, read, mark, learn, and inwardly digest them, that by patience and comfort of your holy Word, we may embrace and ever hold fast the blessed hope of everlasting life, which you have given us in our Saviour Jesus Christ. *Amen.*

(Collect: Advent 2)

Almighty God, whose Word is a lantern unto our feet, keep us resolute and steadfast in the things that cannot be shaken; and help us to lift up our eyes and behold, beyond the things that are seen and temporal, the things that are unseen and eternal; through Jesus Christ our Lord. *Amen.*

The Lord's Prayer.

HYMNS: *Christ is made the sure Foundation.*
Thou art the Way: by thee alone.

PERCEPTION

Aim: The eternal world is not some far-off sphere beyond the stars; heaven is very close; it interpenetrates the material universe in which we live; it touches us at every point. The temporal is but the outer cloak of the eternal. But it is necessary that we train our eyes not only to 'see' but to 'perceive'. Jesus brings this home in his parable about a pearl merchant. The merchant knew what he was looking for so that when he came across a pearl of great value he was able to recognise it for what it was.

Illustration:
A painting discovered in a boys' remand home in Manchester became one of the most expensive paintings at auction when it fetched two and a half million dollars (£1,168,224) at Sotheby's in New York.

The painting was *Icebergs* by the 19th century American artist Frederick Edwin Church, which had been lost for over one hundred years. A huge canvas, measuring five feet by nearly ten feet, it was known to exist, but all attempts by art historians to find it had failed.

It came to light recently when the superintendent of the boys' home, Rosehill in Northenden, Manchester, wanted to find cash to buy and renovate a derelict cottage in the Pennines for the boys.

'The painting had been hanging on the wall for years,' said Mr Glen Baulch, the superintendent. 'Then my wife, Mira, had the idea of selling it. But she had no idea it was worth anything like this.'

The painting was dirty. Workmen had placed ladders against it and it had been used as a dartboard. One boy had added his signature alongside that of the artist. Although most people in Britain have never heard of Church, to Americans he is the greatest 19th century landscape artist.

Icebergs was bought in the 19th century by an MP, Thomas Watson, on behalf of a railway magnate, Sir Edwin William Watkin, who owned Rosehill. The house was sold to the city in 1910.

READING:
St Matthew 13. 45, 46. 'Here is another picture of the kingdom of Heaven. A merchant looking out for fine pearls found one of very special value; so he went and sold everything that he had, and bought it.'

O gracious and holy Father,
 Give us wisdom to perceive thee,
 intelligence to understand thee,
 diligence to seek thee,
 patience to wait for thee,
 eyes to behold thee,
 a heart to meditate upon thee,
 and a life to proclaim thee;
through the power of the Spirit of
 Jesus Christ our Lord. *Amen.*

(St Benedict, 480–543)

The Lord's Prayer.

HYMNS: *Teach me, my God and King.*
   Mine eyes have seen the glory of the coming of the Lord.

13

FAITH

Aim: Faith is not 'taking a deep breath, closing your eyes and swallowing something.' It is, rather, a mental activity similar to what we recognise as a diagnosis in medicine. It has to do with observing and assembling facts and then leaping through them to the truth that underlies and unifies them.

Illustration:
Lord Hailsham tells us:
 There had been no exact moment when my belief in religion had failed, but the point at which I realised that it had wholly disappeared was the day upon which my mother died.
 I was at Eton, and I was seventeen years of age. It happened that I was in bed with influenza. My brother, Edward Marjoribanks, came into the room, unexpected and unannounced. "I have bad news for you," he said, "mother died this morning." She had died of a stroke, and I had not expected it. Nothing quite so awful, indeed nothing really awful at all,

24

had happened to me before, for mine had been a fairly protected childhood. In the afternoon the headmaster came in to comfort me. He was a gentleman, and a Christian. He sought to console me with talk about the after-life. I was discourteous. I suddenly realised that I did not believe a word of what he was saying, and I told him so. I said that I believed that when we died we were nothing. "Like the animals," I said, for good measure. He was angry and went away.'

Later, when faith returned, Lord Hailsham writes: 'You do not get out of your philosophical troubles arising out of the fact of evil by rejecting God. For, as I have tried to point out before, the real problem is not the problem of evil, but the problem of good; not the problem of cruelty and selfishness, but the problem of kindness and generosity; not the problem of ugliness, but the problem of beauty. If the world is really the hopeless and meaningless jumble which one has to believe it to be if once we reject our value judgements as nothing more than emotional noises, with nothing more in the way of objective truth than a certain biological survival value for the species rather than the individual, evil then presents no difficulty because it does not exist. We must expect to be knocked about a bit in a world which consists only of atoms, molecules and strange particles. But how, then, does it come about that we go through life on assumptions which are perfectly contrary to these facts, that we love our wives and families, thrill with pleasure at the sight of a little bird discreetly dressed in green and black and white, that we rage at injustice on innocent victims, honour our martyrs, reward our heroes, and even, occasionally and with difficulty, forgive our enemies, and do good to them that persecute us and despitefully use us? No, it is light which is the problem, not darkness. It is seeing, not blindness. It is knowledge, not ignorance or error. It is love, not callousness. The thing we have to explain in the world is the positive, not the negative. It is this which led me to God in the first place. It is this which leads me to think that I know something about his activity in the world through the Christ of history.'

(The Door Wherein I Went by Lord Hailsham)

READING:
> *Job 28. 12–28.*
> 'But where can wisdom be found?
> And where is the source of understanding? . . .
> The fear of the Lord is wisdom,
>   and to turn from evil is understanding.'

PRAYER:

> O gracious and holy Father,
> Give us wisdom to perceive thee;

Intelligence to understand thee;
Diligence to seek thee;
Patience to wait for thee;
Eyes to behold thee;
A heart to meditate upon thee;
And a life to proclaim thee,
Through the power of the Spirit of Jesus Christ, our Lord

Amen.

(*St Benedict, 480–543*)

The Lord's Prayer.

HYMNS: *O for a faith that will not shrink.*
Forth in thy name, O Lord, I go.

14

THE NATURE OF LOVE

Aim: 'The love I speak of is not our love for God, but the love he showed to us in sending his Son as the remedy for the defilement of our sins.' *(1 John 4. 10)*

Illustration:
Jimmy loved to gaze through the window of his local sweet shop as he made his way home from school each day. The choice, the shapes, the colours, were enough to make any child's mouth water. His favourites, however, were the pink and white marshmallows which seemed to bulge inside their cellophane packs. But the price was completely beyond his reach – 25 pence a pack!

He gave the matter a lot of thought and gradually an idea began to form. One afternoon after he had eaten his tea, he went up to his room and carefully wrote a little note to his mother which read as follows:

Dear Mummy,

I enclose the following account:

Cleaning Shoes	5 pence
Going Shopping	8 pence
Feeding the Dog (three days at 2 p. a day)	6 pence
Washing Up	2 pence
Helping to lay the Table	4 pence
TOTAL:	25 pence

26

He placed the note in an envelope and addressed it to his mother. Before going up to bed that evening he left the envelope on the sideboard where he knew his mother would see it.

The following morning when he came down to breakfast, he glanced at the sideboard and saw the envelope where he had left it, with his mother's name crossed out and his own written in its place. He opened the envelope and to his joy he found 25 pence inside, together with the following note:

Dear Jimmy,

Enclosed, 25 pence and many thanks for your help. May I also submit my account:

Feeding and Clothing for 11 years	No pence
Nursing through measles, chicken pox, etc.	No pence
Transport to Scout Cubs, Judo, Parties and numerous other activities over the years	No pence
Cost of Entertainment for 11 years	No pence
TOTAL:	No pence

Jimmy suddenly felt that he didn't want any marshmallows! Twenty-five pence was suddenly an embarrassment and he put it in his money box to hide it away. And I just feel that maybe he had learnt quite a lot about the true meaning of love.

(George Hill. Llandaff Cathedral School)

READING:

1 Corinthians 13. 1–13. 'I may speak in tongues of men or of angels, but if I am without love . . . When I was a child, my speech, my outlook, and my thoughts were all childish. When I grew up, I had finished with childish things. Now we see only puzzling reflections in a mirror, but then we shall see face to face. My knowledge now is partial; then it will be whole, like God's knowledge of me. In a word, there are three things that last for ever: faith, hope, and love; but the greatest of them all is love.'

PRAYER:

Heavenly Father,
  We thank you
    For those whose love and care and service and
    understanding we so often take for granted.
  Graft into our hearts that love
    Which is always happier to give than to get;
    Which is always eager to help and always ready to
    forgive;
    Which is always sensitive to the needs of others.
      And now:

To God the Father, who first loved us, and made us accepted
in the Beloved;
To God the Son, who loved us, and washed us from our sins in
his own blood;
To God the Holy Spirit, who sheds the love of God abroad within
our hearts;
Be all love and all glory
For time and for eternity.
Amen.

The Lord's Prayer.

HYMNS: *Love divine, all loves excelling.*
Give me joy in my heart, keep the praising.

15

MERCY

Aim: The Hebrew word for Mercy is 'Chesedh' and it means having the
the ability to get right inside the other person's skin until we can
see things with his eyes, think things with his mind, and feel things
with his feelings. It is sympathy which leads to action. (It is no use
just feeling sorry for someone and doing nothing about it.)

Illustration:
It was the custom for the Religious Dramatic Society in the village of
Great Shelford, near Cambridge, to produce a nativity play every Christ-
mas in their beautiful village church.

In 1943 they produced a play called *Holy Night.* The story was about a
statue of the Virgin Mary coming to life in a splendid cathedral in Spain.
Stepping down from her plinth, surrounded by the richly vested cathedral
clergy, she makes her way to the great west door. They try to prevent her;
she pauses and tells them that she wishes to join the poor, the wretched,
the sad and the humble who have to live in the squalor of the slums outside the cathedral walls.

Near Great Shelford at that time was a prisoner-of-war camp, full of
young German soldiers. The parishioners of Great Shelford decided that

it would be a fitting gesture to invite the prisoners to a special performance of the play.

The camp commandant agreed to let the men come; but he insisted that they had to march to the church; there was to be no transport.

They came in a dreary sort of way. The camp discipline had been very strict. There was a great number of them, and they filled the church. The atmosphere was dull and lifeless; they were not expecting anything; they were just obeying orders.

Before the play began one of the villagers with a limited knowledge of German tried to give them some idea of the plot, but he did not make a very good job of it.

The play got under way, but clearly the audience wasn't very interested. Then the moment came when the young girl taking the part of the Virgin Mary 'came to life' and stepped down from her plinth. When the others tried to stop her, she paused and began her speech, but not in English – in German.

Knowing who her audience would be on that night, she had taken the trouble of learning her speech in German. It transformed the whole atmosphere, the play leapt to life.

At the end, everyone stood to sing *Holy Night* in their own tongue. The joy and the beauty of the Christmas message swept through the church. Men had come in as prisoners; they went out 'free'.

(Rosemary Essex in The Church Times)

READINGS:

St Luke 10. 30–37. 'A man was on his way from Jerusalem down to Jericho when he fell in with robbers, who stripped him, beat him, and went off leaving him half dead. . . .'

St Matthew 5. 7. 'How blest are those who show mercy; mercy shall be shown to them.'

PRAYER:

Holy Father:
Help us to be thoughtful and sensitive to the needs of others;
Help us to welcome the stranger and to see that the shy are not left out of things;
Help us to uphold the weak and strengthen the faint-hearted;
Help us to remember that sympathy which does not lead on to action is of little worth.
We ask this in the name of our example and Saviour
Jesus Christ.
Amen.

The Lord's Prayer.

HYMNS: *When I needed a neighbour, were you there?*
If I had a hammer, I'd hammer in the morning.

16

THE IMMEASURABLE

Aim: With slide-rules, computers, microscopes, balances and every conceivable electronic device, we measure and calculate in order to discover the vital statistics and, we hope, the truth about things. But we must remember that we are also surrounded by immeasurables which defy analysis and measurement, for example, beauty, love, loyalty, courage, sacrifice, grief – the list is long. It is to this category of the immeasurable that religion belongs. People say, you cannot 'prove' that God exists. But how can you prove or measure beauty or courage? You cannot, but that doesn't mean they don't exist.

Any quantity surveyor could tell us all about the vital statistics of this church/school we are in. He could tell us about its height, its length, its breadth, the tonnage of its mortar and stone. But how could anyone measure the role this church/school has played in the history of our nation?

It would be a simple matter to measure the length, breadth and thickness of the memorial plaque and to give a chemical analysis of the material from which it is made. But who could measure the sacrifice made by the young men whose names are written on it, and who could measure the grief experienced by the parents who have stood in front of it?

Illustration:
Consider the following formula for a female.
A woman is made up of:
4 ounces of sugar;
50 quarts of water;
3 pounds of calcium;

2 ounces of salt;
Sufficient chlorine to disinfect a swimming pool;
Enough sulphur to rid a dog of fleas.

But who would pretend that such an analysis is adequate? Let us go to the poet Sir Walter Scott who writes:
'Oh Woman! in our hours of ease,
Uncertain, coy, and hard to please,
And variable as the shade
By the light quivering aspen made;
When pain and anguish wring the brow,
A ministering angel thou!'

READINGS:

Psalm 8. '. . .When I look up at thy heavens, the work of thy fingers, the moon and the stars set in their place by thee, what is man that thou shouldst remember him. . . .? Yet thou hast made him little less than a god crowning him with glory and honour. . . .'

Romans 8. 31–39. 'With all this in mind, what are we to say? If God is on our side, who is against us? He did not spare his own Son, but gave him up for us all . . . It is Christ – Christ who died, and, more than that, was raised from the dead – who is at God's right hand, and indeed pleads for our cause. . . . I am convinced that there is nothing in death or life, in the realm of spirits or superhuman powers, in the world as it is or the world as it should be, in the forces of the universe, in heights or depths – nothing in all creation that can separate us from the love of God in Christ Jesus our Lord.'

Isaiah 40. 12–31. 'What likeness will you find for God or what form to resemble his?. . . . To whom then will you liken me, whom set up as my equal?. . . . Lift up your eyes to the heavens; consider who created it all . . .'

PRAYER:

O God, we recognise in you the master-mind behind all being, behind the universe. We thank you for the designed pattern of order and relationships in the far distant galaxies and in the atom itself.

We thank you not only for the pattern behind the universe, but for the plan behind the pattern and the purpose behind the plan.

We thank you not only for the mind that planned, but for the love that gave and revealed the plan.

We thank you for the mind becoming man in Christ, and for the purpose beyond space and time that has reached us through him.

In whose name we offer you these our thanksgivings. *Amen.*

(David Ingram)

The Lord's Prayer.

HYMNS: *Immortal, invisible, God only wise.*
God of concrete, God of steel.

17

BEING REAL

Aim: What is being real? We become real when we are loved. Loved by our family, loved by our friends, and above all, loved by God.

Illustration:
The Skin Horse had lived longer in the nursery than any of the others. He was so old that his brown coat was bald in patches and showed the seams underneath, and most of the hairs in his tail had been pulled out to string bead necklaces. He was wise, for he had seen a long succession of mechanical toys arrive to boast and swagger, and by-and-by break their mainsprings and pass away, and he knew that they were only toys, and would never turn into anything else. For nursery magic is very strange and wonderful, and only those playthings that are old and wise and experienced like the Skin Horse understand all about it.

'What is *real*?' asked the Rabbit one day, when they were lying side by side near the nursery fender, before Nana came to tidy the room. 'Does it mean having things that buzz inside you and a stick-out handle?'

'*Real* isn't how you are made,' said the Skin Horse. 'It's a thing that happens to you. When a child loves you for a long, long time, not just to play with, but *really* loves you, then you become Real.'

'Does it hurt?' asked the Rabbit.

'Sometimes,' said the Skin Horse, for he was always truthful. 'When you are Real you don't mind being hurt.'

'Does it happen all at once, like being wound up,' he asked, 'or bit by bit?'

'It doesn't happen all at once,' said the Skin Horse. 'You become. It takes a long time. That's why it doesn't often happen to people who break easily, or have sharp edges, or who have to be carefully handled. Generally, by the time you are Real, most of your hair has been loved off, and your eyes drop out and you get loose in the joints and very shabby. But these things don't matter at all, because once you are Real you can't be ugly, except to people who don't understand.'

'I suppose *you* are Real?' said the Rabbit. And then he wished he had not said it, for he thought the Skin Horse might be sensitive. But the Skin Horse only smiled.

'The Boy's Uncle made me Real,' he said. 'That was a great many years ago; but once you are Real you can't become unreal again. It lasts for always.'

(The Velveteen Rabbit by Margery Williams)

READINGS:

1 John 4. 7–12. 'Dear friends, let us love one another, because love is from God. . . . The love I speak of is not our love for God, but the love he showed to us in sending his Son as the remedy for the defilement of our sins. If God thus loved us, dear friends, we in turn are bound to love one another. . . .'

St John 3. 16. 'God loved the world so much that he gave his only Son, that everyone who has faith in him may not die but have eternal life.'

St John 15. 11–17. 'This is my commandment: love one another, as I have loved you.'

PRAYER:

Holy Father,
We thank you for the love you showed us by sending your Son to
    live with us.
We thank you for the love he showed towards his fellow-men,
    the love which led him to the cross.
We thank you for the love of our families and our friends.

Give us O God
The love which is always ready to forgive others;
The love which is always eager to help;

33

The love which is always happier to give than to get;
The love which sets us apart as followers of your Son Jesus Christ
our Lord. *Amen.*

The Lord's Prayer.

HYMNS: *Come down, O Love divine.*
My song is love unknown.

18

LOYALTY

Aim: There is nothing quite like loyalty. No worth-while relationships can be established without it. Nothing arouses our admiration more than when we see it in action. Nothing is quite so disappointing and pathetic when we see it fail.

Illustration:
During one of his campaigns, Alexander the Great entered his tent and found an unsigned letter lying on his table. It contained a warning that his physician had been bribed to introduce a lethal dose of poison into his next cup of medicine. He had scarcely finished reading the letter when the physician appeared carrying a goblet. He placed it on the table before Alexander and indicated that it was time for the draught to be taken. For a moment Alexander considered the cup and then lifting it to his lips he drained it to the very dregs. Having done so, he handed the letter to the physician.

Of course, the cup had not been poisoned. But Alexander had demonstrated beyond all question the extent of his trust in the physician's loyalty by drinking the medicine first before asking him to read the letter. In short, Alexander showed by that act that he would rather be dead than be betrayed by someone he trusted.

READINGS:
Ruth 1. 16, 17. 'Where you go, I will go, and where you stay, I will stay. Your people shall be my people, and your God my God. . . . nothing but death shall divide us.'

34

2 Samuel 15. 16–23. 'The king said to Ittai the Gittite, "Are you here too? Why are you coming with us? . . ." "As the Lord lives, your life upon it, wherever you may be, in life or in death, I, your servant, will be there." '

PRAYER:
O God, you have made our hearts such that loyalty is the most precious quality in this life. Help us to have this loyalty.
Help us to have loyalty to our principles, so that everyone may know where we stand and what we stand for.
Help us to have loyalty to the truth, so that everyone may know that our word can be trusted, absolutely.
Help us to have loyalty to our friends, so that we will never let them down, and so that they can be certain that we will stand by them in any company and in any circumstances.
Help us to be loyal to our loved ones and to be true to them through all the chances and the changes of this life.
Help us to be loyal to you, so that we will never be ashamed to show whose we are and whom we serve, so that we shall be proud to let the world see that for us Jesus Christ is Lord.

Amen.

The Lord's Prayer.

HYMNS: *O loving Lord, who art for ever seeking.*
Rise up, O men of God.

19

PRESERVING A SENSE OF WONDER

Aim: As our understanding of the created order deepens and increases, we must guard our sense of wonder and mystery.

Illustration:
When we consider the simplicity of some basic unit of the universe such as the hydrogen atom, and the fact that its potential for change is apparently limited to the rise and fall of its energy level, to the greater or lesser

35

excitation of its components, and reflect that with this were made the humming-bird and the whale, the mind of an Aristotle, an Einstein, a Kierkegaard, the music of Handel and the utterance of Shakespeare, the Wiltshire downs and the green mountains of Vermont, Michelangelo's David and the courage of good men, no miracle, no portent, can ever arouse more wonder than the fact of the natural order and the mystery of the human soul.

(The Foolishness of God by John Austin Baker)

READINGS:

Psalm 104. '. . . . O Lord my God, thou art great indeed, clothed in majesty and splendour, and wrapped in a robe of light.
Thou has spread out the heavens like a tent and on their waters laid the beams of thy pavilion;
who takest the clouds for thy chariot, riding on the wings of the wind;
who makes the winds thy messengers and flames of fire thy servants. . . .
Thou makest grass grow for the cattle. . . .
The trees of the land are green and leafy,
the cedars of Lebanon which he planted;
the birds build their nests in them,
the stork makes her home in their tops.
High hills are the haunt of the mountain-goat,
and boulders a refuge for the rock-badger.
Thou has made the moon to measure the year and taught the sun where to set. . . .
I will sing to the Lord as long as I live,
all my life I will sing psalms to my God.
May my meditation please the Lord,
as I show my joy to him!'

'To see a World in a Grain of Sand,
    And a Heaven in a Wild Flower,
Hold Infinity in the palm of your hand,
    And Eternity in an hour.'

(Auguries of Innocence by William Blake)

PRAYER:

Lord of the Universe, open our minds that we may see your presence in all that surrounds us:
    In the joy of loving and being loved,
    In the laws revealed by science,

36

In the beauty of hedgerows, fields and trees,
In the homeliness of familiar roads and streets and buildings,
In the majesty of mountains and tranquility of lakes,
In the might of the storm, and the awesomeness of the
	thunder cloud.
In the delicacy and loveliness of small flowers and insects.

Amen.

Lord of infinite greatness, who hast ordered and adorned in equal perfection all that thou hast made; who hast set in glorious array the eternal heavens, and yet dost paint the lily that abideth but a day; give us courage to attempt great things in thy name, and equal faithfulness to do the small; to thy sole honour and glory, through Jesus Christ our Lord.

Amen.

The Lord's Prayer.

HYMNS: *O Lord of every shining constellation.*
Morning has broken, like the first morning.

20

GLORY

Aim: The word 'Glory' when used technically within a religious context means 'reflection'. To glorify means to reflect. It is the role of God's people to reflect God in the World and at the same time reflect the love of God back to God.

Illustration:
One of the greatest aids to motorists who drive at night is the cat's eye reflector. The idea started with a Yorkshireman, Peter Shaw, who regularly drove at night from Bradford to Halifax. The road along which he travelled had many a dangerous twist and turn. When visibility was bad, motorists depended on the glow of their headlights shining on the tram lines which linked the two towns.

One wet foggy night Peter Shaw set out as usual, but was somewhat taken aback when he found that there were no tram lines to guide him; they had been taken up. He had to proceed very cautiously. As he approached one particularly dangerous bend, he suddenly saw in front of him two bright pin-points of light shining through the fog. He realised as he drew closer that they were the eyes of a cat sitting on the fence.

Peter Shaw thought a lot about the incident and eventually devised a lens which was protected by a rubber cap and sealed into a copper ferrule. This in turn was mounted in a cast-iron case and sunk into the middle of the road.

Since then, millions of 'cat's eyes' have been produced and used on all our principal highways. It is a brilliant invention based on the simple principle of reflection that makes our highways much easier and safer to use, especially when visibility is bad.

READINGS:

St Matthew 5. 14–16. 'You are light for all the world. . . . And you . . . must shed light among your fellows, so that, when they see the good you do, they may give praise to your Father in heaven.'

St John 17. 1–5. '. . . Father, the hour has come. Glorify thy Son, that the Son may glorify thee. . . . This is eternal life; to know thee who alone are truly God, and Jesus Christ whom thou hast sent. I have glorified thee on earth by completing the work which thou gavest me to do. . . .'

PRAYER:

Dear Lord Jesus, grant that we may be given power to reflect you in our lives:
Where there is hatred let us reflect your love;
Where there is unrest let us reflect your serenity;
Where there is boasting and pride let us reflect your humility;
Where there is cowardice let us reflect your courage;
Where there is cheating let us reflect your honesty;
Where there is sadness and sorrow let us reflect your joy;
Where there is doubt let us reflect your faith.   *Amen.*

The Lord's Prayer.

HYMNS: *Father, Lord of all Creation.*
Eternal Ruler of the ceaseless round.

21

UNDERSTANDING

Aim: We should always respect what others hold sacred, especially if we wish to live in harmony with them. Difficulties often occur because we do not understand. There is an 'apocryphon' attributed to Josephus which tells us that forty years after the crucifixion of Jesus, when the Romans captured Jerusalem in AD 70, a band of soldiers headed for the Holy of Holies which stood in the very heart of the Temple. Determined to find out what lay inside, they tore down the veil which hid the interior from mortal gaze and were amazed to find that there was absolutely nothing there! They couldn't understand it!

Illustration:
This man of the early race, therefore, she told me, dearly loved his black and white cattle. He always took them out into the veld himself, chose the best possible grazing for them, and watched over them like a mother over her children, seeing that no wild animals came near to hurt or disturb them. In the evening he would bring them back to his kraal, seal the entrance carefully with branches of the toughest thorn, and watching them contentedly chewing the cud, think, 'In the morning I shall have a wonderful lot of milk to draw from them.' One morning, however, when he went to his kraal expecting to find the udders of the cows full and sleek with milk, he was amazed to see they were slack, wrinkled and empty. He thought with immediate self-reproach he had chosen their grazing badly, and took them to better grass. He brought them home in the evening and again he thought, 'Tomorrow for a certainty I shall get more milk than ever before.' But again in the morning the udders were slack and dry. For the second time he changed their grazing, and yet again the cows had no milk. Disturbed and suspicious, he decided to keep a watch on the cattle throughout the dark.

In the middle of the night he was astonished to see a cord of finely woven fibre descending from the stars; and down this cord, hand over hand, one after another came some young women of the people of the sky. He saw them, beautiful and gay, whispering and laughing softly among themselves, steal into the kraal and milk his cattle dry with calabashes. Indignant, he jumped out to catch them but they scattered cleverly so that he did not know which way to run. In the end he did manage to catch one; but while he was chasing her the rest, calabashes and

39

all, fled up to the sky, withdrawing the cord after the last of them so that he could not follow. However, he was content because the young woman he had caught was the loveliest of them all. He made her his wife and from that moment he had no more trouble from the people of the sky.

His new wife now went daily to work in the fields for him while he tended his cattle. They were happy and prospered. There was only one thing that worried him. When he caught his wife she had a basket with her. It was skilfully woven, so tight that he could not see through it, and was always closed firmly on top with a lid that fitted exactly into the opening. Before she would marry him, his wife had made him promise that he would never lift the lid of the basket and look inside until she gave him permission to do so. If he did a great disaster might overtake them both. But as the months went by, the man began to forget his promise. He became steadily more curious, seeing the basket so near day after day, with the lid always firmly shut. One day when he was alone he went into his wife's hut, saw the basket standing there in the shadows, and could bear it no longer. Snatching off the lid, he looked inside. For a moment he stood there unbelieving, then burst out laughing.

When his wife came back in the evening, she knew at once what had happened. She put her hand to her heart and looking at him with tears in her eyes, she said, 'You've looked in the basket.'

He admitted it with a laugh, saying, 'You silly woman. You silly, silly creature. Why have you made such a fuss about this basket? There's nothing in it at all.'

'Nothing?' she said, hardly finding the strength to speak.

'Yes, nothing,' he answered emphatically.

At that she turned her back on him, walked away straight into the sunset and vanished. She was never seen on earth again.

To this day I can hear the old black servant woman saying to me:

'And do you know why she went away, my little master? Not because he had broken his promise but because, looking into the basket, he had found it empty. She went because the basket was not empty; it was full of beautiful things of the sky she stored there for them both, and because he could not see them and just laughed, there was no use for her on earth any more and she vanished.'

(The Heart of the Hunter by Laurens van der Post)

READING:

> *St Matthew 27. 45–51.* 'From midday a darkness fell over the whole land. . . . Jesus again gave a loud cry, and breathed his last. At that moment the curtain of the temple was torn in two from top to bottom.'

(Note: up to this time God had been hidden and remote, and no man knew what he was like. But in the death of Jesus we see the hidden love of God. The life and death of Jesus show us what God is like, and removes for ever the veil which hid God from men.)

'There is a vacuum in every man which only God can fill.'

PRAYER:
Give us, O God, thoughtfulness, imagination and patience to discover why other people feel and think and behave as they do, so that our understanding may grow and our sympathy deepen. Show us how to use our insight to help our friends, our companions and our enemies, in the spirit of him whose knowledge of human nature was as deep as life itself, Jesus Christ our Lord. *Amen.*

(Marlborough College)

The Lord's Prayer.

HYMNS: *Immortal, invisible, God only wise.*
The God who rules this earth gave life to every race.

22

GRACE

Aim: Grace is a free and unearned gift from God; a gift which transforms us into creatures of spiritual loveliness. It is something which shines out from within, and has nothing to do with what we wear however precious or beautiful it may be.

Illustration:
In days long past there lived in the East a man who owned a most valuable ring which was given him by someone he loved very dearly. The stone in the ring was an opal, which shone all colours of the rainbow, and it had a magic power which made anyone who wore the ring and believed in it, much loved by God and man. So the owner did not take off the

41

ring, and he made sure that it would, on his death, go to his best-loved son who should then pass it on in the same way.

But in time it belonged to a man who had three sons whom he loved equally. He just could not choose between them and, perhaps in loving weakness, he promised each one of them, 'You will have this wonderful ring.' But as he grew older, he worried . . . What could he do about the ring? Whichever son had it, the others would be hurt . . .

He thought of a plan. He sent for a goldsmith in secret and ordered two more identical rings. They were so much alike, even he could not tell the difference between them and the real one. He brought each son before him and gave each one a ring and his blessing.

But when their father died, the sons each produced a ring and claimed to be the new head of the family. Eventually, they went to a judge, who told them: 'Each of you shall hold his ring to be the real one, and therefore you must compete to make the ring's power visible. You must show humility, tolerance and be devout. And if the stone's power shows itself in your children, let them come back to the court. Until then, let a wiser man than I sit here and give judgement.'

(As told by Len Goss)

READING:

> *Ephesians 3. 14–19.* '. . . that out of the treasures of his glory he may grant you strength through his Spirit in your inner being, that through faith Christ may dwell in your hearts in love . . . . to grasp, with all God's people, what is the breadth and length and height and depth of the love of Christ . . . .'

PRAYER:

> May 'the peace of God, which is beyond our utmost understanding . . . keep guard over your hearts and thoughts, in Christ Jesus.' May '. . . all that is true, all that is noble, all that is just and pure, all that is loveable and gracious, whatever is excellent and admirable – fill your thoughts . . .' And may 'the grace of our Lord Jesus Christ be with your spirit.'

(Philippians 4. 7, 8 and 23)

The Lord's Prayer.

HYMNS: *Come down, O Love divine.*
Lord of all hopefulness, Lord of all joy.

23

'LOVE ONE ANOTHER!'

Aim: 'If he does not love the brother whom he has seen, it cannot be that he loves God whom he has not seen. And indeed this command comes to us from Christ himself: that he who loves God must also love his brother.'

(1 John 4. 20–21)

Illustration:
Abou ben Adhem, (May his tribe increase!)
Awoke one night from a deep dream of peace,
And saw within the moonlight in his room,
Making it rich and like a lily in bloom,
An Angel, writing in a book of gold.
Exceeding peace had made ben Adhem bold,
And to the Presence in the room he said,
'What writest thou?' The Vision raised its head
And with a look made of all sweet accord,
Answered, 'The names of those who love the Lord.'
'And is mine one?' said Abou. 'Nay not so,'
Replied the Angel. Abou spoke more low
But cheerily still, and said, 'I pray thee, then,
Write me as one who loves his fellow-men.'
The Angel wrote and vanished. The next night
He came again with a great wakening light,
And showed the names whom love of God had blessed
And lo! ben Adhem's name led all the rest.

(James Leigh Hunt)

READINGS:
St Matthew 25. 31–46 '. . . I tell you this: anything you did for one of my brothers here, however humble, you did for me.'

St Luke 10. 25–37. 'On one occasion a lawyer came forward to put this test question to him . . . . who is my neighbour? Jesus replied, "A man was on his way from Jerusalem down to Jericho . . ."'

Heavenly Father,
We ask you to give us that grace which will make us sensitive
to the needs of others.
Let your Holy Spirit flow through us,
so that we may never refuse an appeal for help,
so that we may find our joy in service and not in
selfishness, in giving and not in getting; in sharing and
not in keeping.
Help us to set a Christian example wherever we are and to
reflect in our lives that love which Jesus came to reveal.
Amen.

The Lord's Prayer.

HYMNS: *When I needed a neighbour, were you there?*
Sing we a song of high revolt.

24

MOTHER TERESA OF CALCUTTA

Aim: A witness is one who knows and is therefore able to tell or
proclaim. Those who have been baptized into Christ are under his
command to: 'Go forth to every part of the world, and proclaim
the Good News to the whole creation.'

(Mark 16. 15)

Illustration:
The day begins for the Sisters with prayers and meditation at 4.30 a.m.
followed by Mass. After the Mass they do their washing and other chores
with great vigour. Everything is done vigorously. They each have a
shining bucket, which is pretty well their only possession, apart from their
habits and devotional books. Then comes breakfast, after which they go
off to their various outside duties – some to the Home for the Dying,
some to schools and dispensaries, some to the lepers, and some to look
after the unwanted babies and children who come into their charge in

increasing numbers as it becomes known that, however overworked they may be, and however overcrowded the available accommodation, none will ever be refused.

Accompanying Mother Teresa, as we did, to those different activities for the purpose of filming them – to the Home for the Dying, to the lepers and unwanted children – I found I went through three phases. The first was horror mixed with pity, the second compassion pure and simple, and the third, reaching far beyond compassion, something I had never experience before – an awareness that these dying and derelict men and women, these lepers with stumps instead of hands, these unwanted children, were not pitiable, repulsive or forlorn, but rather dear and delightful; as it might be, friends of long standing, brothers and sisters. How is it to be explained – the very heart and mystery of the Christian faith? To soothe those battered old heads, to grasp those poor stumps, to take in one's arms those children consigned to dustbins, because it is his head, as they are his stumps and his children, of whom he said that whosoever received one such child in his name received him.

For those of us who find difficulty in grasping with our minds Christ's great propositions of love which make such dedication possible, someone like Mother Teresa is a godsend. She is this love in person; through her we can reach it, and hold it, and incorporate it in ourselves. Everyone feels this. I was watching recently the faces of people as they listened to her – just ordinary people who had crowded into a school hall to hear her. When she finished and the meeting was over, they all wanted to touch her hand; to be physically near her for a moment; to partake of her, as it were. She looked so small and frail and tired standing there giving herself. Yet this, I reflected, is how we may find salvation. Giving, not receiving. One old man, not content just to take her hand, bent his grey head down to kiss it. So they do to queens and eminences and great seigneurs. In this particular case, it was a gesture of perfect thankfulness to God – in which I shared – for helping our poor stumbling minds and fearful hearts by showing us his everlasting truth in the guise of one homely face going about his work of love.

(Something Beautiful for God by Malcolm Muggeridge)

READINGS:

St Matthew 28. 16–20. 'Full authority in heaven and on earth has been committed to me. Go forth therefore and make all nations my disciples . . . .'

James 2. 14–17. 'My brothers, what use is it for a man to say he has faith when he does nothing to show it? . . . . So with faith; if it does not lead to action, it is in itself a lifeless thing.'

Christ has no body now
on earth but yours.
No hands but yours,
No feet but yours;
Yours are the eyes
through which is to look out
Christ's compassion to the World;
Yours are the feet
with which he is
to go about doing good;
Yours are the hands
with which he is
to bless us now.
Amen.

(St Teresa of Avila)

The Lord's Prayer.

HYMNS: *Kumbaya, my Lord, Kumbaya.*
Take my life, and let it be.

25

A MARTYR (Mother Maria)

Aim: The term 'martyr' is a Greek word which means 'a witness'. The term was originally used of the Apostles as witnesses of Christ's life and resurrection, but with the spread of persecution it was reserved for those who had undergone hardships for the faith, and finally it was restricted to those who had suffered death.

Illustration:
Mother Maria was born into a wealthy landowning family in Russia in 1891. From an early age she sympathised with the poor and oppressed and was appalled by the wretched circumstances under which so many of the ordinary people were forced to live.

46

In those days she was known as Elizabeth Pilenko. When the Russian revolution took place in 1917 she and millions of others looked forward to a just society being founded where freedom and justice would be established and where equality and fraternity would lead on to happiness and prosperity. But sadly things did not turn out that way, men and women continued to live in fear, and freedom of expression was repressed.

Disappointed with the turn of events, Elizabeth Pilenko left her beloved Russia, never to return. She went to Paris where she became a nun, and took the name of Maria. She identified herself completely with the poor of that great city, caring for the sick, visiting the old and infirm and teaching the little children.

As the years passed, she managed to collect enough money to open a small hospital for those who were in desperate need of being nursed, and a few nuns joined her.

In 1940, the German army overran France, and the whole country was placed under German control. Soon, as they were doing in other countries, the Nazis began to hunt out all Jews, packing them into cattle trucks and sending them off to be exterminated in their terrible concentration camps. Millions and millions of men, women and children were starved, tortured and eventually gassed in their specially constructed gas chambers.

As soon as the Nazis began to arrest Jews in Paris, Mother Maria let it be known secretly, that she was prepared to hide them in her hospital and arrange escape routes for them. For a while her plan worked successfully, but then someone gave the show away and she was arrested and sent immediately to Ravensbruck, one of the very worst of all the concentration camps. Here she was submitted to the same awful conditions as the other prisoners, but she was not gassed because she was not a Jew. Mother Maria immediately seized on her new situation to comfort, to reassure and generally minister to the suffering humanity in that hell-hole.

Such was her love towards her fellow-men that even the brutalised guards whose daily work was to torture and gas people, respected and revered her.

And then, one day, some women prisoners were lined up outside the gas chamber. A young girl, realising what was about to happen to her, lost her nerve and began to scream and cry hysterically.

Two guards moved forward threateningly, but Mother Maria, who happened to be near at hand, ran forward, and put her arm around the girl's shoulders and kissed her.

'Don't be frightened,' she said. 'Look, I shall come in with you.'

And she went into the gas chamber with the girl, a smile of great peace and happiness on her beautiful face.

It was Good Friday, 1945.

The war ended a few weeks later.

(*The Nun in the Concentration Camp by G. W. Target. Abridged*)

READINGS:

Romans 8. 31–39. '. . . Then what can separate us from Christ? Can affliction or hardships? Can persecution, hunger, nakedness, peril, or the sword? . . . . For I am convinced that there is nothing in death or life, in the realm of spirits . . . in heights or depths – nothing in all creation that can separate us from the love of God in Christ Jesus our Lord.'

The Wisdom of Solomon 2. 1–5 and 3. 1–9 (*Apocrypha-A.V.*).
'. . . Our life is short and tedious, and in the death of a man there is no remedy: neither was there any man known to have returned from the grave . . . . our body shall be turned into ashes, and our spirit shall vanish as the soft air, and our name shall be forgotten in time, and no man shall have our works in remembrance, and our life shall pass away as the trace of a cloud, and shall be dispersed as a mist, that is driven away with the beams of the sun, and overcome with the heat thereof . . . But the souls of the righteous are in the hand of God and there shall no torment touch them. In the sight of the unwise they seemed to die: and their departure is taken for misery, and their going from us to be utter destruction: but they are in peace. For though they be punished in the sight of men, yet is their hope full of immortality. . . . As gold in the furnace hath he tried them, and received them as a burnt offering. And in the time of their visitation they shall shine, and run to and fro like sparks among the stubble. . . .'

PRAYER:

O Lord Jesus Christ,
> Help us to be your witnesses in the world;
> Help us to show whose we are and whom we serve;
> Grant that our lives may shine like lights
> in the dark places of this world, and help
> us to lead others to you.
> We thank you that this life is not the end,
> That we are preparing ourselves for another and greater life,
> That there is a place where all questions will be answered,
> and all hopes realised;

That we will meet again those whom we have
loved and lost awhile.
Amen.

The Lord's Prayer.

HYMNS: *For all the saints who from their labours rest.*
Thine be the glory, risen, conquering Son.

26

TAKING NOTICE OF PEOPLE

Aim: A kind word, a smile, a friendly gesture can transform somebody's
day. So why don't we distribute them with complete generosity?
After all, we have a limitless supply!

Illustration:
Many years ago, in a happy country far away, everyone was given at
birth a small soft Fuzzy Bag. Any time a person reached into this bag he
was able to pull out a Warm Fuzzy. Warm Fuzzies were very much in
demand because whenever someone was given a Warm Fuzzy it made
him feel warm and fuzzy all over. People who didn't get Warm Fuzzies
regularly were in danger of developing a sickness in their backs which
caused them to shrivel and die.

In those days it was easy to get Warm Fuzzies. Any time that
somebody felt like it, he might walk up to you and say, 'I'd like to have a
Warm Fuzzy.' You would then reach into your bag and pull out a Fuzzy
the size of a little girl's hand. As soon as the Fuzzy saw the light of day it
would smile and blossom into a large, shaggy, Warm Fuzzy. You then
would lay it on the person's shoulder or head or lap and it would snuggle
up and melt right against their skin and make them feel good all over.
People were always asking each other for Warm Fuzzies, and since they
were always given freely, getting enough of them was never a problem.
There were always plenty to go round and as a consequence everyone was
happy and felt warm and fuzzy most of the time.

One day a bad witch became angry because everyone was so happy and
no one was buying her potions and salves. This witch was very clever and

49

she devised a very wicked plan. She crept up to citizens of this happy land who were freely giving away Fuzzies. 'You know,' she said, 'if you keep this sort of thing up eventually you are going to run out of Fuzzies and there won't be any left for you.' This was very clever, for it had never occurred to anyone before that Fuzzies could be used up. But now the idea scared people, even though they found a Warm Fuzzy every time they reached into their bags. They reached in less and less and became more and more stingy. Soon people began to notice the lack of Warm Fuzzies, and they began to feel less and less fuzzy. They began to shrivel up and, occasionally, people would die from lack of Warm Fuzzies. More and more people went to the witch to buy her potions and salves even though they didn't seem to work.

The situation was getting very serious indeed. The bad witch who had been watching all this didn't really want the people to die so she devised a new plan. She gave everyone a bag that was very similar to the Fuzzy Bag except that this one was cold while the Fuzzy Bag was warm. Inside the witch's bag were Cold Pricklies. These Cold Pricklies did not make people feel warm and fuzzy, but made them feel cold and prickly instead. But, they did prevent peoples' backs from shrivelling up. So from then on, every time somebody said, 'I want a Warm Fuzzy,' people who were worried about depleting their supply would say, 'I can't give you a Warm Fuzzy, but would you like a Cold Prickly?' Sometimes, two people would walk up to each other, thinking they could get a Warm Fuzzy, but one or other of them would change his mind and they would wind up giving each other Cold Pricklies. The end result was that while very few people were dying, a lot of people were still unhappy and feeling very cold and prickly.

So the situation was very, very dismal; and it all started because of the coming of the witch who made people believe that some day, when least expected, they might reach into their Warm Fuzzy Bags and find no more.

(A fairy tale by Claude M. Steines. Amended)

READING:

Colossians 3. 12–17. 'Then put on the garments that suit God's chosen people, his own, his beloved: compassion, kindness, humility, gentleness, patience. Be forbearing with one another, and forgiving. . . . To crown all, there must be love, to bind all together. . . . Let the message of Christ dwell among you in all richness. . . . Whatever you are doing, whether you speak or act, do everything in the name of the Lord Jesus. . . .'

50

O God,
   Help us to be thoughtful and sensitive in our encounters with
   people;
   Help us to be generous in distributing words of encourage-
   ment, smiles of acknowledgement and acts of goodwill;
   Help us to make people feel that they matter;
   Help us at all times to reflect the nature of Jesus in our lives.
                                                        Amen.

The Lord's prayer.

HYMNS: *O thou who camest from above.*
        Forth in thy name, O Lord, I go.

27

ONLY ONE TALENT

Aim: Those of us who seem to be ungifted mustn't shrug our shoulders
and give up. We have all got at least one talent. It is important that
we use this talent and develop it to the utmost. For example, we all
have the capacity to help others, to cheer people up, to show
people that we care. These are precious talents.

Illustration:
Long ago there lived a tumbler who travelled from fair to fair across the
countryside, earning his livelihood entertaining the crowds. He was very
skilled and always drew large numbers of spectators who loved to watch
him juggling with plates and clubs and balls and performing all sorts of
breath-taking acrobatics.

At the height of his powers, he fell sick and managed to make his way
to a monastery where he was nursed back to health.

The tumbler was so impressed with the love and care lavished on him
by the monks that he decided he too would like to become a monk.

He asked to see the Abbot.

'Reverend Father,' he said, 'I would like to become a member of your
community.'

51

'Very well, my son,' replied the Abbot, 'we shall be happy to let you join us as a novice. At the end of twelve months we shall see how you have managed to settle in.'

The tumbler was placed under the guidance of a senior monk, called the Novice Master, who was responsible for the training of beginners.

'Now,' said the Novice Master, 'we shall start you off in the Library. I know that the librarian has been short-handed and would like some help.'

The Novice Master introduced the tumbler to the librarian and left him in his charge. But the tumbler didn't know the first thing about manuscripts and couldn't read Latin, the language in which the manuscripts were written. He turned out to be more of a hindrance than a help, although he tried very hard. Eventually the librarian went to see the Novice Master.

'You must take him away,' he pleaded, 'he is totally unsuited for any work in the Library.'

The Novice Master took the tumbler to the Scriptorium where he was given some writing material and a quill pen, and some simple copying work to do. But he had difficulty in holding the pen and made mistake after mistake. After less than a week he had to be moved.

The tumbler was taken to the Chapel and left with the choir-master, in the hope that he might be trained as a singer. The choir-master persevered for many weeks, but in the end he gave up.

'You must take him away,' he begged, 'he's ruining every service. I've never met anyone so unmusical.'

Next he was transferred to the kitchens. But here again, try as he might, he made mistake after mistake. He forgot to add salt when boiling vegetables. He burnt the meat. He used the wrong pots and pans. After a month the chef called on the Novice Master.

'You must take that tumbler away from the kitchen,' he said in desperation. 'He means well and he tries hard. But he is completely chaotic. Nothing is in its proper place, and I just don't know what calamity to expect next.'

He was transferred from the kitchens to the farm, from the farm to the dispensary, from the dispensary to the wine-cellars; but the story was always the same.

'Please take the tumbler away from here, he's a nice man, he tries hard, we all like him, but – please move him somewhere else.'

The twelve months passed by and the tumbler knew that his interview with the Abbot regarding his suitability was drawing near.

'I'm a failure,' he thought to himself sadly. 'I have no gift to offer God like the other monks. I can't sing; I can't write; I can't read Latin; I can't cook; I can't mix herbs for medicine; I'm useless. O God,' he prayed, 'I wish I had a gift I could offer you.'

52

At that moment a marvellous idea swept into his mind. 'I know what I'll do,' he said to himself, and hurried off to the Chapel.

He walked up the length of the Chapel and stood in front of the altar and bowed low. Then, removing his habit, he began to tumble. He went through his whole range of acrobatics with tremendous skill, and juggled balls, plates and clubs faster than the eye could see.

During the performance, one of the monks happened to enter the Chapel, and saw the tumbler in action. He rushed off to the Abbot's study. Bursting in, he gasped, 'Father Abbot, come quickly. The tumbler has gone out of his mind. He's gone mad! He's performing acrobatics in the Chapel, in front of the altar of all places!'

The Abbot accompanied the monk to the Chapel. There, sure enough, the tumbler was giving the exhibition of his life, with an expression of pure joy on his face. The Abbot stood and watched. The monk plucked his sleeve and whispered urgently, 'Aren't you going to put a stop to this dreadful behaviour in the Chapel?'

'Sh'sh!' replied the Abbot, putting his finger to his lips, and continued to watch with evident pleasure.

After a while the Abbot turned, and beckoning to the monk, quietly left the Chapel.

'Father Abbot!' protested the monk, 'why didn't you stop that man and reprimand him for behaving so irreverently in God's presence?'

'Ah,' said the Abbot with a gentle smile, 'you don't understand, do you? Can't you see that the tumbler is offering the only thing he is good at to God? And, what's more, I'm sure that God is delighted with his offering!'

A few days later when the tumbler appeared before the Abbot, he was surprised by the warmth of his welcome.

He really expected to be told that he wasn't suited to the life of the monastery.

Instead he heard the Abbot say to him, 'If you still wish to stay with us, you are very welcome. I am sure that we shall all enjoy being entertained by you from time to time. It will be quite a change having a tumbler as one of our members.'

READING:

> *St Matthew 25. 14–30.* '. . . to one he gave five bags of gold, to another two, to another one, each according to his capacity. . . . The man who had the five bags went at once and employed them in business, and made a profit of five bags, and the man who had the two bags made two. But the man who had been given one bag of gold went off and dug a hole in the ground, and hid his master's money . . . .'

Holy Father:
Help us to discover within ourselves the gifts you have given us;
Help us to remember that these gifts can only be developed through
    perseverance and self-discipline.
Help us to be the sort of people who always try to put something
    into life and not to be the sort of people who are forever trying
    to get something out of life.
Help us always to keep a look-out for people to whom we can be
    of use; so that we may carry on the work of our Lord and
    Master Jesus Christ.
Amen.

The Lord's Prayer.

HYMNS: *Awake, my soul, and with the sun.*
Teach me, my God and King.

28

TAKING THINGS FOR GRANTED

Aim: We must beware of taking so much for granted.

Illustration:
As the industrial towns of Britain grew like mushrooms during the
nineteenth century, their citizens lived in squalid overcrowded conditions.
One of their greatest hazards was the threat of epidemic disease such as
smallpox or typhus. Perhaps the most dreaded of all was Asiatic cholera
which reached England in 1831. Cholera soon struck hard and
repeatedly. The first epidemic took 52,000 lives. Worse was to follow in
1848, with a death toll of 53,000 in England and Wales alone; it came
again in 1854, when over 20,000 people died of the disease. These cold
figures are bad enough, but they were all the more frightening because no
one knew what caused cholera or how it spread.

A few doctors of medicine started to investigate the patterns of death.
Dr Shapter was one of the first to do so, in Exeter (1849). By placing
dots on the map of the city, each showing houses where people had died

of cholera, he found that the most dangerous streets and alleys all lay in the lowest parts of the city, close to the river, where drainage was bad. Why that should be so, it was impossible to say. An essential piece of this deadly jigsaw puzzle was still missing.

It was found by a young London doctor, John Snow, in 1854. When he plotted the locations of cholera deaths in that epidemic, he saw that over five hundred people died in ten days in a small area of Soho. They all drank water from an old pump in Broad Street, and Snow realised that it was polluted with sewage. The cholera 'bug' was carried in dirty water.

He had the handle of that pump removed, and no fresh cases were reported from Soho. A similar piece of brilliant detective work was done in the city of Oxford by Dr Henry Acland. It was splendid to know how to prevent cholera, but there was still a long way to go in curing those poor people who did catch it.

(*The Cholera Detectives by F. V. Emery*)

READING:

2 *Samuel 23. 13–17.* '. . . One day a longing came over David, and he exclaimed, "If only I could have a drink of water from the well by the gate of Bethlehem!". . . .'
(David was a fugitive on the run from the Philistines. As he drank the stale, tainted water from his leather bottle, he longed for the sweet, fresh water – which as a boy he had taken for granted – from the well in Bethlehem.)

PRAYER:

Holy Father we thank you:
For life-giving water and wholesome food;
For our homes, our families and our friends;
For freedom of speech and just laws;
For those who wage war on disease and pain;
For the lives and examples of the good and brave of every age;
Above all we thank you for the life on earth of Jesus our example who came to show us how to live. *Amen.*

The Lord's Prayer.

HYMNS: *Thankyou for ev'ry new good morning.*
Let us, with a gladsome mind.

29

INNOCENCE OF MIND

Aim: 'With the holy thou shalt be holy: and with a perfect man thou shalt be perfect.
With the clean thou shalt be clean: and with the froward thou shalt learn frowardness.' (*Psalm 18. 25, 26, as in the Book of Common Prayer*)

Illustration:
One Saturday, Don Camillo, the parish priest, decided to go to the market at La Villa, seven miles away, and soon ate up the miles on his old bicycle. But when he came out of a shop, his bicycle, which he had left leaning against the wall, had disappeared. He decided not to make any fuss, pulled his hat over his eyes and started to walk home. At a certain point along the road there was a small brick bridge, and leaning up against the wall was his bicycle. He knew every inch of it and there was no chance of any mistake. He looked over the wall and saw a man sitting on the river-bank. The man stared up at him inquiringly.

'This bicycle is mine,' Don Camillo said with a little hesitation.

'What bicycle?'

'The one here against the wall of the bridge.'

'Good,' said the man. 'If there's a bicycle on the bridge and it's your bicycle, that's not my business.'

'I was just telling you,' Don Camillo said with considerable perplexity. 'I don't know how it got here.'

The man laughed. 'It must have got bored waiting and gone on ahead of you,' he said. 'Are you, as a priest, able to keep a secret?'

'Certainly,' said Don Camillo.

'Then I can tell you that I found your bicycle in front of the shop and I took it.'

Don Camillo opened his eyes wide.

'I meant to take it for keeps. Then I thought better of it and pedalled after you. I followed you and then took a short-cut, got here before you and put it right under your nose.'

Don Camillo sat down on the wall.

'Why did you take a bicycle that wasn't yours?' he asked.

'Everyone to his own trade. You deal in souls and I deal in bicycles.'

'Where are you going now?' asked Don Camillo.

'Back to see if there's anything doing at La Villa.'

'To see if you can lay hands on another bicycle?'
'Of course.'
'Then keep this one.'
The man looked at him.
'Not on your life, Father. Not even if it were made of solid gold. It would be on my conscience and ruin my career. I prefer to stay clear of the clergy.'

Don Camillo asked if he had had anything to eat, and the man said no.

'Then come and eat something with me.' Don Camillo hailed a passing wagon, and said to the man: 'Come along, you wretch, you bring the bicycle to my house and I'll go in the wagon.'

The man came up from below the bridge: he was so angry that he threw his cap on the ground and cursed a large number of saints before he got on the bicycle . . .

Don Camillo had the meal ready by the time the bicycle thief arrived. 'There's only bread, sausage, cheese and a drop of wine,' said the priest. 'I hope that's enough for you.'

After an hour or so, the man said he must be off, but there was a worried look on his face. 'I don't know how I can go back to stealing bicycles,' he sighed. 'You've demoralised me completely.'

'I'll tell you what,' said Don Camillo, 'I'll take you on as a bell-ringer. Mine just went away two days ago.'

'But I don't know how to ring bells.'

'A man who knows how to steal bicycles won't find that hard to learn.'

And he was bell-ringer from that day on.

(The Bicycle by Giovanni Guareschi)

READING:

St Matthew 5. 8. 'How blest are those whose hearts are pure; they shall see God.'

(The Greek word *Katharos* (pure) means 'unmixed', 'unadulterated', 'unalloyed'. Used in the above way it can describe innocence of mind.

PRAYER:

Holy Father,

Help us to see the good in others, even when it is difficult to see.

Help us to forgive others, even when it is difficult to forgive.

Help us to find our joy in giving and not in getting;
in sharing and not in keeping.

Help us at all times to reflect the innocence and love of Jesus
in our lives. *Amen.*

The Lord's Prayer.

HYMNS: *Blest are the pure in heart.*
Come, thou Holy Spirit, come.

30

ECOLOGY

Aim: The writer of the first chapter of the Book of Genesis brings his account of creation to a close by telling us that God gave man rule over the created order. If man is to fulfil that trust he must cultivate an ever deepening respect for the environment and be more protective of all forms of life.

Illustration:
Of all the beauties of our countryside, the hedges are most often taken for granted. They are so familiar that we scarcely notice them. We don't expect to find much difference between one hedge and the next, and we assume they have always been part of the landscape – so what's in a hedge? The answer is not what you might expect. Some are very old indeed – older than the Norman Conquest of 1066. Others are much younger, but most of them are more than one hundred and fifty years old, and they originated in various ways.

The oldest go back to a time when men planted a hedge so as to make a boundary between two estates. These are generally quite straight. Each landowner dug a ditch along the edge of his property, piled the soil into a bank and planted hawthorns along it. Other hedges are simply the remnants of woodland, or even of the Royal Forests in medieval times, left behind when people cleared the rough ground for cultivation. These twist and turn, and are usually thick with elder, hazel bushes or ash trees.

Others date from Tudor times, when farmers began to enclose the old, open, common fields and changed them into proper, compact farms. After all, the point of having hedges is to keep animals grazing in one field, while alongside it you can grow crops in another field. Hedges stop the two getting mixed up.

Most of our hedges date from the 18th and 19th centuries, when enclosures went ahead by Act of Parliament. They are low, thin, and straight, chiefly of hawthorn, with elms planted along them. So hedges are man-made pointers to agricultural progress in our countryside. Scientists like Max Hooper suggest that if you take a length of thirty-five metres of any hedge, and count the number of species of shrubs and trees you find in it, for every species you can then estimate one hundred years of age for that particular hedge.

Hedges have also become the refuge for many species of wild animals and plants, adding to their practical usefulness an invaluable shelter for Mother Nature's children. For this reason we may regret the destruction of so many hedges by farmers who wish to have bigger fields, so that their mechanical cultivators and combine harvesters have more space in which to operate. In recent years about 5,000 miles of hedges were uprooted each year in Britain. By achieving one objective, we may be creating fresh problems at the same time.

(The Not-so-humble Hedge by F. V. Emery)

READINGS:

Genesis 1. 26, 29 and 30. 'Then God said, "Let us make man in our image and likeness to rule the fish in the sea, the birds of heaven. . . ."*

Psalm 104.

PRAYER:

O God we thank you:
    For the world in which we live;
    For the sun that warms us, and the air that gives us life;
    For all the beauty of the earth in field and hedgerow, woods
        and hills;
    For our rivers, seas and oceans, and all their teeming life.
Heavenly Father give us wisdom so that we may be watchful and worthy stewards of your creation. *Amen.*

The Lord's Prayer.

HYMNS: *For the beauty of the earth.*
       All creatures of our God and King.

31

COVETOUSNESS

Aim: We can spoil our enjoyment of life by longing for what other people have. When we feel like this it is a useful exercise to take stock of our own possessions.
'Count your many blessings, name them one by one,
And it will surprise you what the Lord has done.'

'The man who covets is always poor.' (*Claudian*)

Illustration:
One of John's earliest memories was that of looking across to the other side of the valley in which he lived and admiring a house which had golden windows. Often he would pause in his play and look wonderingly at them and say to himself, 'I wish I lived in a house with golden windows; ours are made of just ordinary glass!'

When John reached his eighth birthday, he was thrilled to find that his parents had bought him a brand new bicycle to replace the one that had grown too small for him. He had never travelled more than half a mile or so from home before, on his own, but now that he was eight, and the proud owner of a new bike, he asked his mother if he might be allowed to ride across to the other side of the valley. Much to his joy, she gave him her permission, with the usual caution to be careful.

'At long last,' he murmured to himself as he swung on to his bike, 'I can have a good close-up view of those golden windows.'

Twenty minutes later he approached the house, and carefully leaving his bike against the hedge, walked up to the boundary fence.

To his surprise he discovered that the windows were not made of gold at all. Far from it! They were made of ordinary glass. He felt let down! Disappointed!

As he walked back to his bycicle he happened to glance in the direction of his own home, clearly visible across the valley, and there he noticed, to his utter astonishment, that the windows of his home gleamed gold in the afternoon sun.

'He who does not know how to be content with what he has is poor, however rich he may be; but he who has learned to be content is rich even though he may have very little. . . . Excessive wants are the seat of suffering; and the labour of weariness of this world of life and death arise from covetousness. He who wants little and so is above the concerns of this life is perfectly free both as to body and mind. . . . Contentment is the domain of wealth and pleasure, of peace and rest. The contented man is happy even though his bed is the bare ground; while the man who knows not the secret of being content is not satisfied even when dwelling in heavenly places.'

(The Buddha)

READINGS:

Exodus 20. 17. (The Tenth Commandment) 'You shall not covet your neighbour's house; you shall not covet your neighbour's wife, his slave, his slave-girl, his ox, his ass, or anything that belongs to him.'

Book of Common Prayer: The Catechism. 'My duty towards my neighbour is . . . not to covet nor desire other men's goods; but to learn and labour truly to get mine own living, and do my duty in that state of life, unto which it shall please God to call me.'

PRAYER:
O God,
Keep us from taking for granted the blessings you have conferred upon us and deliver us from the attitude of mind which envies and resents what others have.

To this end give us the diligence which will never shirk the toil of learning and the discipline which will refuse the easy way. Help us at all times to remember that sweat is the price of all things precious; and give us grace to use to the full the gifts and talents you have given us.

Amen.

The Lord's Prayer.

HYMNS: *Forth in thy name, O Lord I go.*
Give me joy in my heart, keep me praising.

32

THE SABBATH

Aim: 'The Sabbath was made for the sake of man and not man for the Sabbath. . . .' (*St Mark 2. 27*)

61

The fourth commandment had an added significance in an age when there were slaves and servants who had no rights. This commandment decreed that one day in seven must be a day of absolute rest. Otherwise they would have been worked seven days a week, fifty-two weeks a year!

Although we can worship God when we are alone and at any time, worshipping together as the family of God opens up a new and supportive dimension. In order to do this properly a set day must be agreed upon and set aside by society – and what better day for a Christian society than the first day of the week, that weekly reminder of the resurrection of our Lord Jesus Christ from the dead.

Illustration:

The Martian student, swooping low over Britain in his flying saucer, scribbled furiously with his writing tentacle. He had chosen an ideal morning for taking notes, a fine July Sunday, with all the natives coming out of their houses and obligingly spreading themselves around for his observation. But he was in a desperate hurry, he had only one more week in which to complete his thesis!

The report he wrote was brilliant. In several Martian universities, professors have read it out aloud as a shining example of what students should aim at.

'Like so many primitive life forms (thus went the Martian's thesis) the creatures of the third planet are sun worshippers. One day in every seven is set apart for the adoration of their deity – weather permitting. Their rituals vary, and each apparently involves a special form of dress; but all are conducted in the open air; and most seem to require the collection of enormous crowds.

'Some, stripping themselves almost naked in their ecstasy, visit the seashore in great throngs and there perform their rites, oftentimes hurling themselves into the waves with frenzied cries. After the ceremonial immersion, devotees have been observed to anoint themselves with holy oils and stretch themselves at full length with eyes closed, in order to surrender themselves entirely to silent communion with the deity.

'Some, sad to say, practise human sacrifice, the instrument of death being a four-wheeled vehicle which may be employed in various ways. Often, a chosen victim is run down and crushed. More frequently the sacrifice is voluntary; devotees enter the vehicles, and, either work themselves into a frenzy by travelling at high speeds until they dash themselves to bits against other vehicles or stationary objects, or else congregate in vast throngs too closely packed to move, and allow the sun's rays beating upon the hot metal to cook them slowly to death.'

Exodus 20. 8–11. 'Remember to keep the sabbath day holy. You have six days to labour and do all your work. . . . Therefore the Lord blessed the sabbath day and declared it holy.'

Psalm 26. 8. 'Lord, I have loved the habitation of thy house: and the place where thine honour dwelleth.'

Psalm 100. 4. 'Enter into his gates with thanksgiving, and into his courts with praise.'

St Luke 4. 16–20. 'So he came to Nazareth, where he had been brought up, and went to synagogue on the Sabbath day *as he regularly did.* He stood up to read the lesson and was handed the scroll of the prophet Isaiah . . . . and all eyes in the synagogue were fixed on him.'

PRAYER:

Holy Father, Holy God, through the guidance of your Holy Spirit, you have taught your Church to set aside the first day of the week to remind people of the glorious resurrection of your son Jesus Christ from the dead. Teach us to use this day for the worship of your holy name, and the refreshment of our souls and bodies; and help us to make every effort to keep this day holy in the life of our nation; through Jesus Christ our Lord.

Amen.

The Lord's Prayer.

HYMNS: *Praise to the Lord, the Almighty, the King of creation.*
O worship the King.

33

OUR COUNTRY (23 April)

Aim: Wherever we turn, if we have the eye to see and the mind to explore, we can trace our history. A barrow or tumulus on the skyline; a

63

circle of stones; Roman villas; castles; medieval churches; country houses, our language and our literature. Through these we enter into the inner world of the mind, they are the legacies of the spirit which has animated our country over the millennia. And it is only through an understanding of our past that we are better able to comprehend our present.

Illustration:

At one time, not so long ago, historians thought that the bubonic plague had wiped out a handful of medieval villages in England. So severe was the great epidemic of the Black Death, they argued, it must surely have killed off the inhabitants of smaller settlements. There the matter rested until historians of the landscape ('the best document we have', as someone once said) began to find traces of many more 'deserted villages' than was thought to be the case. For one of the features of the English countryside, especially in the Midland counties, is that you sometimes come across a church standing on its own amid the fields. There seems to be no rhyme or reason why it should be there; no farms or cottages, barns, stables, or workshops can be seen at all in the neighbourhood, clustering in the normal manner around the church. Were they once there, and, if so, what happened to them?

When you look down on such places from an aircraft, especially early or late in the day when the low sun casts a long shadow, you see that the ground near the lonely church is broken into a complicated pattern of bumps and hollows. They are the tumbled remains of village buildings, which once housed an active farming community. Alerted by such clues, searchers after the lost villages have succeeded in plotting well over two thousand of them in England, many more than was thought possible. Sometimes a single big farm, and an old church that may now be used no longer, are all that mark a thriving place recorded as far back as Domesday Book in 1086.

Why should so many villages disappear in the 15th and 16th centuries, because that was when they drop out of the records? Why should they be so very plentiful in some regions of England, and so rare in others – which could hardly be the case if they were uniformly the casualties of the Black Death? The answer seems to lie in a less spectacular but more finally destructive set of reasons. Instead of having lots of village tenants who ploughed the land and grew crops in their fields, the landlords turned to running their property with sheep and cattle, which needed fewer men to look after them. Ploughing was replaced with grazing, corn gave way to grass, and (as one observer said) 'the sheep began to eat up the men'.

It is worth remembering, as we walk through our familiar landscapes, that features – even whole villages – may vanish from them as well as be added to them.

(Lost Villages in England by F. V. Emery)

READINGS:

Psalm 90. (BCP)

'Lord, thou has been our refuge: from one generation to another.

Before the mountains were brought forth, or ever the earth and the world were made: thou art God from everlasting, and world without end . . . .

For a thousand years in thy sight are but as yesterday: seeing that is past as a watch in the night.

As soon as thou scatterest them they are even as a sleep: and fade away suddenly like the grass.

In the morning it is green, and groweth up: but in the evening it is cut down, dried up, and withered . . . .

The days of our age are threescore years and ten; and though men be so strong that they come to fourscore years: yet is their strength then but labour and sorrow; so soon passeth it away, and we are gone . . . .

So teach us to number our days: that we may apply our hearts unto wisdom . . . .'

'Lives of great men all remind us
We can make our lives sublime,
And, departing, leave behind us
Footprints on the sands of time.'

PRAYER:

O God, grant us a vision of our land, fair as she might be; a land of justice, where none shall prey on others; a land of plenty, where vice and poverty shall cease to fester; a land of brotherhood, where all success shall be founded on service, and honour shall be given to nobleness alone; a land of peace, where order shall not rest on force, but on the love of all for the land, the great mother of the common life and weal. Hear thou, O Lord, the silent prayer of all our hearts, as we pledge our time and strength and thought to speed the day of her coming beauty and righteousness. *Amen.*

(Walter Rauschenbusch)

The Lord's Prayer.

HYMNS: *And did those feet in ancient time.*
Lord of lords and King eternal.

34

TREES

Aim: 'That it may please thee to give and preserve to our use the kindly fruits of the earth, so as in due time we may enjoy them; we beseech thee to hear us, good Lord.'

(Book of Common Prayer. From The Litany)

Illustration:

Only an eye sated with too much print or too many electronic images is blind to the forest's infinitely varied colours. Only the ear dulled by the city's rumble is deaf to the forest's distinct utterance. Only the nose blunted by the city's fumes will not perceive the astringent whiff of conifer, the honeyed fragrance of blossom, the chaste scent of lichen. Only the hand numbed by soft living can fail to distinguish, even in darkness, the separate feel of the cedar's smooth webbing, the rough texture of the fir.

Any man of average intelligence will see that the forest has a sixth sense of its own. When countless millions of cells multiply by sure plan and long-tested architecture; when roots thinner than silk and strong as steel never cease their quest for moisture and hidden chemical; when pumps and capillary plumbing, which man has yet to invent or understand, carry the liquid upward to synthesize the tree's food by means unknown and exude the oxygen of all animal life; when trunk and limb swell and spread as if an engineer had designed them for stress and strain; when the forest, without eyes, unerringly finds the sun and burrows in the dark; when, mindless, it knows how to heal its wounds and rear its children; when, anchored to the earth, it marches generation by generation to recover its lost domain and expunge its human conqueror; when, indeed, the forest defies all laws and logic known to humans, then, perhaps, man witnesses a kind of knowledge totally different from his own, a latent intelligence which, some day, he may learn to share. So far, he has only learnt how to destroy it.

(The Far Side of the Street, Bruce Hutchison)

READINGS:

Genesis 1–2. 2. 'In the beginning of creation, when God made heaven and earth. . . . Then God said, "Let the earth produce fresh growth, let there be on the earth plants bearing seed, fruit-trees bearing fruit each with seed according to its kind." So it was;

the earth yielded fresh growth, plants bearing seed according to their kind and trees bearing fruit each with seed according to its kind; and God saw that it was good . . . .'

'When I can go just where I want to go,
There is a copse of birch-trees that I know;
As in Eden Adam walked with God,
When in that quiet aisle my feet have trod,
I have found peace among the silver trees,
Known comfort in the cool kiss of the breeze
Heard music in its whisper, and have known
Most certainly I was not alone!'
(The Birch Copse, Father Andrew)

PRAYER:
For the strength and peace of the trees,
We thank thee, our God:
For their quiet unhasting growth,
For their stalwart and trusting friendship,
For their sociable neighbourly silence:
For their ancient calm on a windless day:
For their cheery, murmurous stir
When the breeze is abroad with its melodies:
For the quiet and sure revelation of thee
Which they bring to our souls
As we sit thus silent amongst them,
We thank thee, our God.
(John S. Hoyland)

The Lord's Prayer.

HYMNS: *All things bright and beautiful.*
For the beauty of the earth.

35

INDIFFERENCE (Good Friday)

Aim: One of the greatest obstacles facing the Church in this country is indifference, which shows itself as a form of benevolent neutrality.

This will only change when people cease to think of the Church as being made up of a number of people who happen to be interested in religion, a sort of spiritual Rotary Club, and see it as the Body of Christ through which he speaks and through which he acts. And this will only happen when people begin to say of us Christians, 'We will go with you because we have heard that God is with you.'   (*Zechariah 8. 23*)

Illustration:

When Jesus came to Golgotha they hanged him on a tree,
They drove great nails through hands and feet, and made a Calvary;
They crowned him with a crown of thorns, red were his
        wounds and deep,
For those were crude and cruel days, and human flesh was cheap.
When Jesus came to Birmingham, they simply passed him by,
They never hurt a hair of him, they only let him die;
For men had grown more tender, and they would not give
        him pain,
They only just passed down the street, and left him in the rain.
Still Jesus cried, "Forgive them for they know not what they do."
And still it rained the wintry rain that drenched him through
        and through;
The crowds went home and left the streets without a soul to see,
And Jesus crouched against a wall and cried for Calvary.
                        (*The Unutterable Beauty. G. A. Studdert Kennedy*)

READING:

St Mark 15. 21–32. 'Then they took him out to crucify him . . . . they fastened him to the cross. . . . The passers-by hurled abuse at him. . . . "Come down from the cross and save yourself!" . . . "He saved others," they said, "but he cannot save himself. . . ." Even those who were crucified with him taunted him.'

Lamentations 1. 12. 'Is it of no concern to you who pass by? If only you would look and see: is there any agony like mine, like these my torments with which the Lord has cruelly punished me in the day of his anger?'

PRAYER:

Holy Jesus, you allowed yourself to be betrayed, rejected, denied and forsaken; to be accused, condemned, scourged, spat upon and crowned with thorns; to hang in agony on the cross, to die and to be buried so that we might enter into the Kingdom of God. Grant

that we may never be indifferent towards you. Grant that we may
be given power to reflect your love and proclaim the Good News
of your Kingdom. Wherever we are help us to be immediately
recognisable as your followers.
Amen.

The Lord's Prayer.

HYMNS: *Lift high the Cross.*
I danced in the morning when the world was begun.

36

EASTER

Aim: '. . . He has broken the power of death and brought life and
immortality to light through the Gospel.'   (*2 Timothy 1. 10*)

Illustration:
The Bamboo Tree stood tall and straight, holding up its head proudly
because it knew it was the master's favourite plant. Its tall, straight stems
with their thick bunches of waving leaves were far taller than he was.
When the master walked in the garden, the bamboo tree would bow its
proud head in greeting.

One day, the master stood before the bamboo tree and said: 'Bamboo,
bamboo, I'm going to cut you down.'

'Cut me down! Oh no, master, no!'

'Yes. You cannot serve me unless you let me cut you down.'

The bamboo tree bowed its head sadly. 'Very well, master. Cut me
down if that is the only way I can serve you.'

'That is the only way,' said the master. So he cut the bamboo tree
down.

The next day, the master stood looking at the proud bamboo tree lying
on the ground, its stems long and straight and its leaves spread out.

'Bamboo, bamboo,' said the master, 'I must cut off your leaves, all of
them.'

'Very well,' said the bamboo. 'Cut off all my leaves for I would serve
you.'

The bamboo tree lay alone for a time, thinking sadly of all its lost beauty and wondering what else the master had in store for it. Presently, the master returned and said: 'Bamboo, bamboo, you are fine and strong and straight. I shall split you in half from top to bottom and take your core.'

'Oh no, master, no,' wailed the bamboo tree. 'I shall die if you do that. I will serve you any way I can, but do not split me.'

'Bamboo, bamboo, you cannot serve me unless I split you in two and take out your core.'

'As you will, master,' whispered the bamboo tree. So the master split the bamboo from end to end and took out the core. Then he laid the two halves of the stem end to end and fastened them firmly together. One end he laid at the mouth of a little spring of water which bubbled out of the ground and lost itself among the moss and stones. The other end he placed in his rice field, which was parched and dry. Soon the clear spring water was running down from the spring, down the channel made by the bamboo stem, into the dry rice field, bringing refreshment to the drooping, dry plants.

So the bamboo tree died and brought new life to the master's rice field. The rice grew tall and strong and brought life to many people.

(As told by the Rev'd H. S. Colchester)

READINGS:

St Mark 15. 21–16. 8. 'Then they took him out to crucify him. . . . Then Jesus gave a loud cry and died. . . . So Joseph brought a linen sheet, took him down from the cross . . . . laid him in a tomb . . . and rolled a stone against the entrance. . . . On the Sunday morning, just after sunrise, they came to the tomb . . . . and saw that the stone . . . had been rolled back. . . . "Jesus of Nazareth . . . . has been raised again. . . ." '

Romans 6. 5–11. 'For if we have become incorporate with him in a death like his, we shall also be one with him in a resurrection like his. . . .'

PRAYER:

Heavenly Father we thank you for the love of your son Jesus Christ.

We thank you that he offered his life for us on the cross.

We thank you that by his death he has destroyed the power of death and won for all who believe in him everlasting life.

We thank you that he is with us always and that nothing in life or in death can separate us from him. *Amen.*

The Lord's Prayer.

HYMNS: *This joyful Easter-tide.*
Thine be the glory, risen, conquering Son.

37

EMMANUEL—GOD IS WITH US

Aim: 'For I am convinced that there is nothing in death or life, in the realm of spirits or superhuman powers, in the world as it is or the world as it shall be, in the forces of the universe, in heights or depths – nothing in all creation that can separate us from the love of God in Christ Jesus our Lord.'

(Romans 8. 38, 39)

Illustration:
In April 1916, twenty-eight desperate men stood shivering on the beach of an ice-covered, barren island in the Antarctic. Members of a trans-Antarctic expedition, they had grown numb, weak and sick in an 1,800-mile battle against a wilderness of snow and limitless iceberg – great glacial monsters that had crushed and sunk their ships five months before.

Only a few days previously they had cast off in their three remaining small boats from the drifting flow which had been their home; their leader had laid his course for Elephant Island, south-east of Cape Horn. Now even that dreary refuge had to be abandoned. Gales swept the unsheltered shore; the food supply of penguin meat and seaweed was dangerously low. Freezing, hungry, the men turned again – as they had repeatedly through this nightmarish ordeal – to the man whose courage and calmness had thus far preserved them. They turned to Ernest Shackleton.

'We have got to reach a point where we can get a ship,' he said.

Five men were chosen to make the journey of nearly 900 miles to South Georgia, in one of the worst seas in the world and in a boat only 22 feet long. One of the greatest small-boat journeys in marine history was about to begin. Those in the boat knew they might never reach inhabited land; those who stayed knew that if the boat did not succeed they were doomed.

71

The long seas tossed the boat, and the wind bit coldly. Every swell lifted the boat dizzily upwards until they could see for miles in all directions – an unending series of watery grey hills and valleys. The cold was intense. Ice formed on the boat and had to be cut away, otherwise the boat would have sunk. But no man could stand this ice-chopping for more than four minutes; it was bitter punishment. So chafed were their hands and feet from crawling over the ballast that they bled continually. After a spell at the tiller, the helmsman had to be lifted out of his position and rubbed back to life before being tucked into a sleeping bag.

After surviving these appalling conditions for two weeks and through a miracle of navigation the boat reached South Georgia.

On 19 May 1916 Shackleton and two of his companions, Worsley and Crean, struck out across the glaciers and ice-covered mountains of South Georgia leaving behind three men unfit for travel. They roped themselves together and steered by compass. They found themselves in blind passes; they almost fell into a gigantic chasm, 200 feet deep and 200 feet broad, ripped out by the howling gales.

Finally, they reached a ridge so steep they could sit on it and dangle their legs on either side. Fog and darkness had cut off retreat. If they did not move, they would freeze to death. Cutting steps down the icy mountain-side would be so slow as to be useless. So Shackleton declared 'It's a devil of a risk, but we've got to take it. We'll slide.'

Each clasped the one in front and with Shackleton in the lead they kicked off. They shot down the slope at a mile a minute. Eventually, little by little, their speed slackened and they finished up at the bottom in a snowdrift.

The trio eventually reached a whaling station and safety after crossing South Georgia in thirty-six hours. Their three companions were rescued and so were all the men who had been left on Elephant Island. Later, in his book Shackleton wrote: 'When I look back on those days, I have no doubt that Providence guided us. . . . I know that, during that long and racking march of thirty-six hours over the unnamed mountains and glaciers of South Georgia, it seemed to me often that we were four, and not three. I said nothing to my companions on the point; but afterwards, Worsley said to me, "Boss, I had a curious feeling on the march that there was another person with us." Crean confessed the same idea.'

READINGS:
> *Psalm 139. 7–10.*
> 'Where can I escape from thy spirit?
> Where can I flee from thy presence?
> If I climb up to heaven, thou art there;

If I make my bed in Sheol, again I find thee.
If I take my flight to the frontiers of the morning
    or dwell at the limit of the western sea,
even there thy hand will meet me
and thy right hand will hold me fast.'

Acts 27. 9–44. '. . . I urge you not to lose heart; not a single life will be lost, only the ship. For last night there stood by me an angel of the God whose I am and whom I worship. "Do not be afraid, Paul," he said. . . .'

PRAYER:

When the heart is hard and parched up, come upon me with a shower of mercy.

When grace is lost from life, come with a burst of song.

When tumultuous work raises its din on all sides, shutting me out from beyond, come to me, my Lord of silence, with thy peace and rest.

When my beggarly heart sits crouched, shut up in a corner, break open the door, my king, and come with the ceremony of a king.

When desire blinds the mind with delusion and dust, O thou holy one, thou wakeful, come with thy light and with thy thunder.

(*Rabindranath Tagore, Gitanjali*)

HYMNS: *Through all the changing scene of life.*
        Put thou thy trust in God.

38

JESUS CHRIST

Aim: If we want evidence of a miracle, we have but to look at the Church of Christ. Nearly two thousand years on from its lowly beginnings, it is estimated that one-third of the World's population is Christian. In Africa the number of Christians is increasing at such speed that it is likely the whole of the continent south of the Sahara will be Christian by the end of the century. In Brazil the membership of the Church is growing more rapidly than the

73

population. In South Korea membership is increasing at ten per cent per year – more than four times as fast as the population growth! In Burma a new Church is being organised every week. In Indonesia the number of Christians increased from four million in 1964 to eight million in 1970. In India, by 1974, it was estimated that there were fourteen million Christians. On a global scale, the Church is very much on the march!

Illustration:

Here is a man who was born in an obscure village, the child of a peasant woman. He grew up in another village. He worked in a carpener's shop until he was thirty, and then for three years he was a travelling preacher.

He never wrote a book. He never held public office. He never went to college. He never owned a house. He never had a family. He never set foot inside a big city. He never travelled even two hundred miles from the place where he was born. He never did one of the things that usually accompany greatness. He had no credentials but himself. He had nothing to cope with this world except the naked power of his divine manhood.

While he was still a young man the tide of popular opinion turned against him. His friends ran away. One of them denied him. He was turned over to his enemies. He went through the mockery of a trial. He was nailed to a cross between two thieves. While he was dying his executioners gambled for the only piece of property he had while he was on this earth, and that was his coat. When he was dead, he was taken down and laid in a borrowed grave through the pity of a friend.

Nineteen hundred years have come and gone, and today he is the central figure of the human race.

I am far within the mark when I say that all the armies that ever marched, and all the navies that were ever built, and all the parliaments that ever met, and all the kings that ever reigned, put together, have not affected the life of man upon this earth as powerfully as has that *one solitary life.*

READINGS:

Acts 10. 34–43. '. . . He sent his word to the Israelites and gave the good news of peace through Jesus Christ, who is Lord of all. . . . He was put to death by hanging on a gibbet; but God raised him to life on the third day. . . . It is to him that all the prophets testify, declaring that everyone who trusts in him receives forgiveness of sins through his name.'

Colossians 2. 6–10 and 3. 1–4. 'Therefore, since Jesus was delivered to you as Christ and Lord, live your lives in union with

74

him. . . . For it is in Christ that the complete being of the Godhead dwells embodied, and in him you have been brought to completion. . . .' '. . . your life lies hidden with Christ in God.'

Holy Father,
We thank you for the life of Jesus.
We thank you for his teaching and his deeds of love.
We thank you for the courage which made him go to the cross for us.
We thank you that he conquered death, and brought eternal life to all who believe in him.
We thank you for our membership in his universal Church.
Give us the power of your Holy Spirit to show the world whose we are and whom we serve for his dear name's sake.

Amen.

The Lord's Prayer.

HYMNS: *A man there lived in Galilee.*
Alleluia, sing to Jesus.

39

BEREAVEMENT

Aim: 'He who loves more lives than one;
More deaths than one must die.'

It is inevitable that we shall experience sorrow when someone we love dies. Bereavement is bound up in our humanity, it is part of our common lot. We can draw comfort from an immense well of sympathy, because so many have already gone through the experience. The Christian, however, can draw on yet another source of comfort: the message of Easter, that those of us who are in Christ shall be made alive!

'Out of the sleep of earth, with visions rife,
I woke in death's clear morning full of life,

75

And said to God, whose smile made all things bright,
''That was an awful dream I had last night!'' '

Illustration:

Once a beautiful young woman saw her baby child grow sick and die.
The mother went mad with sorrow and clasping the child to her breast
she went from house to house begging the people for a medicine that
would bring her dead baby to life.

Eventually someone sent her to the Buddha. 'Yes,' he said, 'I know of
the proper medicine. It is the ordinary mustard seed.' But, as the young
mother rejoiced at so simple a remedy, he continued, 'You must get it
from some house where no son, or husband, or parent, or slave has ever
died.' *there has been no death.*

The young woman set out on her errand. Wherever she came people
were only too willing to give her the mustard seed. But when she asked,
'Has this house been free from the death of a son, or a husband, or a
parent or a slave?' they replied sadly, 'Such a house is not to be found,
the dead are many and the living few.'

And the young mother, deep in thought, went silently to a forest and
buried her child. When she returned to the Buddha he asked, 'Have you
found the mustard seed?' And the mother replied, 'No my master, but I
have found the medicine. I have buried my sorrow in the forest and now I
am ready to follow you in peace.'

READINGS:

St John 14. 1–6. 'Set your troubled hearts at rest. Trust in God
always; trust also in me. There are many dwelling-places in my
Father's house; if it were not so I should have told you; for I am
going there on purpose to prepare a place for you. . . . I am the
way; I am the truth and I am the life; no one comes to the Father
except by me.'

Romans 8. 18 and 31–39. 'For I reckon that the sufferings we now
endure bear no comparison with the splendour, as yet unrevealed,
which is in store for us. . . . For I am convinced that there is
nothing in death or life, in the realm of spirits or superhuman
powers . . . nothing in all creation that can separate us from the
love of God in Christ Jesus our Lord.'

1 Corinthians 15. 20–26, 35–38, 42–49, 53–57. 'But the truth is,
Christ was raised to life – the firstfruits of the harvest of the
dead. . . . But, you may ask, how are the dead raised? In what
kind of body? . . . If there is such a thing as an animal body, there

is also a spiritual body. . . . As we have worn the likeness of the man made of dust, so we shall wear the likeness of the heavenly man. . . . This perishable being must be clothed with the imperishable, and what is mortal must be clothed with immortality. And when our mortality has been clothed with immortality, then the saying of Scripture will come true: "Death is swallowed up; victory is won!" "O Death, where is your victory? O Death, where is your sting?". . . . God be praised, he gives us the victory through our Lord Jesus Christ.'

1 Thessalonians 4. 13 and 14. 'We wish you not to remain in ignorance, brothers, about those who sleep in death; you should not grieve like the rest of men, who have no hope. We believe that Jesus died and rose again; and so it will be for those who died as Christians; God will bring them to life with Jesus.'

PRAYER:

We thank you, O God, for sending us your Son Jesus Christ.

We thank you that by his death he destroyed the power of death, and by his resurrection opened the kingdom of heaven to all believers.

We thank you that this life is not the end,

That we are preparing ourselves for another and a greater life;

That there is a place where all questions will be answered and all hopes realised;

That we will meet again those whom we have loved and lost awhile.

And now we ask you, Heavenly Father, to deal graciously with those who mourn, that casting their every care on you, they may experience the comfort of your love, through Jesus Christ our Lord. *Amen.*

The Lord's Prayer.

HYMNS: *Christ is made the sure foundation.*
Thine be the glory, risen, conquering Son.

40

THE BODY OF JESUS

Aim: St John in the Prologue to his Gospel writes, '. . . the Word became flesh; he came to dwell among us.' This, Jesus continues to do, in the sense that the Church is the extension of the Incarnation, in which the life of Jesus is continued in the world today. If we fail to recognise this wonderful and sacred mystery, we fail to appreciate what Jesus meant when he promised his disciples, '. . . where two or three have met together in my name, I am there among them.' *(Matthew 18. 20)*

Illustration:
One day a shabbily-dressed man walked into a publisher's office in Moscow. Taking from his pocket a manuscript, he asked that it might be published. The publisher, noticing the stranger's shabby appearance, curtly tossed the manuscript back. Sorry; he had no time to deal with this – even if his client could afford to pay for its publication; which he rather doubted!

'Really,' said the man, 'I must have been misinformed. I am told that people like to read what I write.'

'Indeed,' said the publisher, his curiosity aroused. 'Who are you? What is your name?'

'My name,' said the stranger, as he buttoned up his shabby greatcoat over the rejected manuscript, 'My name is Leo Tolstoy.'

The next minute the publisher was at the other side of the counter, begging the privilege of publishing the manuscript. But the quaint, eccentric genius quietly withdrew with the coveted manuscript in his pocket.

READING:
> *St John 1. 1-14.* 'When all things began, the Word already was. The Word dwelt with God, and what God was, the Word was. . . . He was in the world; but the world, though it owed its being to him, did not recogise him. He entered his own realm, and his own would not receive him. But all who did receive him, to those who have yielded him their allegiance, he gave the right to become the children of God. . . . So the Word became flesh; he came to dwell among us, and we saw his glory, such glory as befits the Father's Son, full of grace and truth.'

Heavenly Father, you have set people apart in every land to be the body of your Son Jesus.

Give us the power to reflect your love into the world so that we may unite the nations into one sacred family, in which justice and mercy, truth and freedom, love and understanding, may flourish and spread.

Grant that we may ever remember the words of St Teresa of Avila:

Christ has no body now
on earth but yours.
No hands but yours.
No feet but yours;
Yours are the eyes
through which is to look out
Christ's compassion to the World;
Yours are the feet
with which he is
to go about doing good;
Yours are the hands
with which he is
to bless us now. *Amen.*

The Lord's Prayer.

HYMNS: *The Church's one foundation.*
Lord Jesus Christ, you have come to us.

79

ACKNOWLEDGEMENTS

The author gratefully acknowledges the following individuals and sources for material reproduced in this book.

JOHN AUSTIN BAKER *The Foolishness of God*
(Darton Longman and Todd)
WILLIAM BARCLAY *Epilogues and Prayers* (SCM Press)
CAMBRIDGE UNIVERSITY PRESS *The New English Bible*
H. S. COLCHESTER
D. J. CONNER
F. V. EMERY
ROSEMARY ESSEX
LEN GOSS
GIOVANNI GUARESCHI *Don Camillo and the Prodigal Son*
(Victor Gollancz Ltd)
LORD HAILSHAM *The Door Wherein I Went* (Collins)
GEORGE HILL
BRUCE HUTCHISON
DAVID INGRAM
RUDYARD KIPLING
HAZEL LLOYD
SIMON LLOYD
MALCOLM MUGGERIDGE *Something Beautiful for God* (Collins)
DONALD O. SOPER
CLAUDE M. STEINER
G. A. STUDDERT KENNEDY *The Unutterable Beauty* (Hodder)
RABRINDRANATH TAGORE
G. W. TARGET *The Nun in the Concentration Camp* (REP)
NORMAN TAYLOR
LAURENS VAN DER POST *The Heart of the Hunter* (Hogarth)
MARGERY WILLIAMS *The Velveteen Rabbit* (Heinemann)

Bible quotations are taken from *The New English Bible* © 1961, 1970 (Oxford and Cambridge University Presses).